Globalization and Indian State

Globalization and Indian State

Education, Health and Agricultural Extension Services in Punjab

Sucha Singh Gill
Sukhwinder Singh
Jaswinder Singh Brar

GLOBALIZATION AND INDIAN STATE
Sucha Singh Gill, Sukhwinder Singh and Jaswinder Singh Brar

First Published 2010

ISBN 978-93-5002-034-0

Published by
AAKAR BOOKS
28 E Pocket IV, Mayur Vihar Phase I, Delhi 110 091
Phone: 011-2279 5505 Telefax : 011-2279 5641
aakarbooks@gmail.com; www.aakarbooks..com

Composed by
Limited Colors, Delhi 110 092

Printed at
Mudrak, 30A, Patparganj, Delhi 110 091

Contents

Preface

The process of globalization is primarily an increasing economic integration of a nation's economy into world economy through the growing volume of cross-border transactions of goods and services; free movement of finance capital, people, ideas and knowledge; and more important, the widespread diffusion of new technology as well as information at an astonishing speed. In a wider perspective, the present phase of globalization has economic, political, technological, and cultural aspects and implications that are interwoven with each other and affect the whole gamut of activities of nation-states. This also calls for liberalization of national markets to allow unrestricted free flow of trade, investments, and profit-earning opportunities within the country and across the national boundaries by facilitating global integration.

The protagonists of globalization presume that full-blown globalization will bring about economic development, employment creation, and prosperity to the majority of the people living in developing countries when free flow of technology transfers and migration of labour/people materialize across the world countries. Globalization is expected to produce the best economic, social and political outcomes for human beings of all nation-states. For the antagonists, the current form of globalization, if pursued vigorously, is very dangerous for the poor or developing nations. They argued that the poor nations have a fragile economic and political power structure, and thereby a weak voice in the international arena. The multilateral trade agreements are favourable to developed nations' commercial interests advanced by the MNCs. It is also held that the contemporary process of globalization is partial and biased because it does not create more employment within the nation. Neither does it allow free movement of labour across the countries. That is why it is argued that there is a need to correct rather than stop the current phase of globalization. Fears are also expressed that globalization will undermine the authority of nation-state and will reduce state's control over vital economic activities.

India entered this phase of globalization in 1991 in the wake of a serious balance of payment crisis. Far-reaching changes were introduced in the major sectors of the economy. These included free entry and exit through de-licensing, relaxing norms for FDI, removal of MRTP Act and Foreign Exchange Regulation Act (FERA), privatization of public enterprises, and opening up of health, education, insurance, banking, infrastructure, roads, and air transport services to the private sector. The economy has been opened to the outside world both for trade of goods and services and for investment by the MNCs. The signing of the WTO agreement in 1994 provided another big boost to the already initiated process of globalization. In an effort to achieve fiscal stabilization, there has been shrinkage in the role of government in running and management of the economy. The government withdrawal has been visible not only in the areas of electricity, oil and natural gas, banking and insurance sectors, but also in the most critical areas of agricultural research and extension, health and education services. In fact, these sectors have been opened up to private players whose main motive is not societal gains but private profits.

The debate on the positive or negative effects of globalization on different sectors of Indian economy, polity and society is going on. The present study examines the effects of globalization on the education, health and agricultural extension services in one of the most advanced and prosperous states of India, i.e. Punjab. This study is a part of the national-level research project entitled *Globalization and the Indian State,* financed and sponsored by the National Foundation for India (NFI), New Delhi. This national-level project was executed by the NFI basically to understand and decipher the impact of globalization on the national economy of India as well as on different sectors of state economies. Formulation of social policy is another aim of this study. Thus, the rationale and significance of the present study is self-evident.

This report is the product of a team effort. The team members developed the overall layout, methodology of study and gave a unified treatment to the main contents of the work. The core members analyzed the secondary data, field observations, and exchanged their notes/contributions in varying degrees; revised/ reformulated them and reorganized the contents, whenever necessary, to make the report a cohesive document without any ambiguity. The study team is responsible for the contents, views and quality of the report.

In completion of this study, many institutions and individuals have extended their valuable cooperation. The team members gratefully acknowledge their contributions in varying degrees. At the forefront of all, Dr. Neera Chandhoke, Professor of Political Science, University of Delhi and Dr. Bhanu P. Mehta, Director, Centre for Policy Research, New Delhi for reposing faith in us by allocating the study. The study team is deeply beholden to them. Ms Vandana Swami from the NFI deserves special thanks as she has contributed in various ways in the timely completion of the study. The study team benefited immensely from mutual discussions during the two conferences arranged by the National Foundation for India, one in November 2005 at India Habitat Centre, New Delhi and the second in October 2006 at Teri Retreat, Gurgaon (Haryana), with all the study teams, discussants and subject experts. The suggestions, comments and observations given by the co-participants proved very useful in the articulation of ideas and enrichment of the final version of the report. The study team greatly acknowledges their academic contribution.

The team is highly indebted to the Vice Chancellor of Punjabi University, Patiala, S. Swarn Singh Boparai, for allowing us to undertake this project and extending all possible help during the various stages of completion. Dr. Parm Bakhshish Singh Sidhu, Registrar, and S. Mohinder Singh, Finance Officer of Punjabi University, Patiala deserve our thanks for their multifarious help. Among the Faculty of Department of Economics, Punjabi University, Patiala, we are highly indebted to Professor Ranjit Singh Ghuman, Professor Inderjeet Singh, Dr. Lakhwinder Singh and Dr. Parmod Kumar for their valuable comments and assistance in crystallizing the thought process and improving the quality of the final report. The help extended by Professor A.S. Joshi, Department of Economics, Punjab Agricultural University, Ludhiana; Mr. Deepinder Singh, PCS, Additional

Secretary Agriculture, Government of Punjab; Er. Balwinder Singh Sidhu, Director of Agriculture; and Mr. Surinder Singh Rair, Statistician (Retd.), Department of Agriculture, Punjab is duly acknowledged.

For the collection of secondary data, the study team searched a large number of published/unpublished reports and approached a number of institutions and libraries located in the region. It is very difficult to reproduce the names of all of them here. The team thanks all of them wholeheartedly. Nevertheless, we would like to mention a few offices of Punjab state here: Economic Advisor, Punjab Government; Director Public Instructions, Punjab; and Director of Agriculture, Punjab. Further, help rendered by the Statistical Officers of Department of Education, Health and Agricultural Extension Services, Punjab is duly acknowledged. The library staff of the following institutions deserves special thanks: Bhai Kahn Singh Nabha Library and Department of Economics Library, Punjabi University, Patiala; A.C. Joshi Library, Panjab University, Chandigarh; Punjab Agricultural University Library, Ludhiana; Jawaharlal Nehru University Library, New Delhi; and State Planning Board Library, and Economic and Statistical Organization Library, both at Chandigarh.

Last but not least, the role of Mr. Surinder Kumar Singla, Research Assistant in the project, deserves appreciation. His contribution is duly acknowledged in the collection of data and in finalizing the report.

Sucha Singh Gill
Sukhwinder Singh
Jaswinder Singh Brar

1
Introduction

1.1 Globalization

The phenomenon of globalization has many aspects and implications. It is referred to as a strategy of economic development where borders of the countries do not matter for movement of commodities, services, capital, finance, technology, ideas and information. This strategy generates a process of increasing economic integration and growing interdependence between countries of the world economy (Nayyar, 1995). The whole emphasis is on development of a global market by removing all sorts of barriers in its way created by governments of countries. In theory, this reinforces the results of the neo-classical theory of international trade in which countries must specialize in the production and export of commodities in which they have a comparative advantage. This is supposed to increase competition between producers of a country with the most efficient producers in the world (Sodersten, 1970). The competition forces the producers of a country to invest in the modern machinery embodying the latest technology. The full-blown globalization is expected to ensure technology transfer and migration among the nations along with the free movement of capital, commodities (both goods and services) and finance.

The process of globalization started on a much wider scale with emergence of capitalism as a universal/dominant system in the world (Amin, 1974). This generated a very powerful wave in the nineteenth century and continued in the twentieth century till the outbreak of the First World War (1870–1914). This was a period when colonialism was at its peak and the developing world of today was occupied as colonies by the imperial powers. This resulted in a high degree of integration of the world economy through international trade and capital investment by imperial powers in the developing countries. The imperial powers enjoyed a preferential position within their colonial empires for foreign trade and capital investment. Consequently, other imperial powers could not compete at an equal level for export of commodities and capital investment in the territory under the control of a particular imperial power. This generated conflict among them (leading to the two world wars) and led to the subordination of the colonial economy to the requirements of imperial powers (Baran, 1958; Amin, 1974; Frank, 1975).

In the post-colonial period, most of the underdeveloped countries adopted a development strategy that consciously attempted to limit the degree of openness and integration with the world economy. This task was attempted through active involvement of the government in development affairs. Many countries adopted a national planning process and tried systematically to protect the domestic producers from competition of well-established global producers. The justification for this came from well-known argument of 'infant industry'. This generated autonomous development and self-reliance in some areas of the economies. It was argued by a number of development economists that the market in these countries was not sufficiently large and developed to allow industrialization in the late comer/erstwhile colonial countries (Rosenstein-Rodan, 1943; Nurkse, 1953; Leibenstein, 1957).

The state was assigned a strategic role for economic development. This was a departure from the colonial era, which was characterized by open economies and unregulated activities. The role of state was considerably enhanced and industrialization strategy had a large component of import substitution (where local/national producers enjoyed a protected market). There was almost a development consensus at that time with very few dissenters. However, this consensus began to face serious challenge in the 1980s from most powerful and influential quarters. The challenge came from the IMF, the World Bank and the US Treasury in the form of an alternative package of policy known as 'Washington Consensus'. Initially, this set of policies was practised by Ronald Reagan in the US and Margaret Thatcher in Britain. These policies are also called 'Neo-liberal' policies. There are three pillars of this consensus. These are: privatization (reducing the role of public enterprises by selling them off), liberalization (freeing up markets from regulation and controls), and macro stability (by controlling fiscal deficit though reduction of government/public spending). These sets of policies were tried in Latin America among the developing countries in the 1980s at the instance of international financial institutions. These institutions spearheaded the implementation of these policies in the countries who were in deep crisis and approaching them (IMF-World Bank) for financial assistance (Stiglitz, 2002; 2003).

The Washington Consensus refers to the development approach which is opposed to the development consensus of the 1950s and 1960s. This has emerged from the integration of traditional concerns of IMF for macroeconomic stabilization (anti-inflation and anti-deficit policies) and the World Bank agenda of efficiency and enhancing reforms (openness, competition, deregulation, and privatization). A typical package includes fiscal and monetary austerity, currency devaluation, trade liberalization, financial liberalization, banking system restructuring, price liberalization, labour market deregulation, tax reforms (especially tax concessions to corporate sector) and subsidy cuts (You, 2002).

The implementation of the Washington Consensus as an alternative strategy of development has been undertaken by the IMF and World Bank with the crucial support of the US treasury. The US has been acting as a key player to enforce this strategy in the world as the largest economy of the globe and leader of G-7 countries. The fall of the Soviet Union and other centrally planned economies and their transition to the market economies in the early 1990s prepared the ground for easy acceptance of these policies in the developing countries. The corporate capitalism led by MNCs played a leading role through media under their control to propagate the relevance of this strategy. An intellectual climate was built where any opposition to this strategy began to be looked upon as orthodox thinking/old-fashioned outlook. MNCs with huge amounts of capital and financial resources at their command and being leaders in technology and human resources have large stakes in this strategy of development (Lall, 2002). They have benefited from the strategy in the form of expansion in the level of their activities and areas of operation. Many virgin areas such as the former Soviet bloc countries, China, Vietnam, etc. came under their operation and accelerated levels of operations in the other areas. The expansions in the level of activities of MNCs accompanied by many concessions extended by the national governments competing for capital and technology of MNCs have made accelerated operations of global giants more profitable.

The formation of WTO replacing GATT since January 1995 has introduced further qualitative and quantitative changes in the process of globalization and contributed to creation of conditions for better implementation of the

Washington Consensus. Many new areas/activities which were earlier not under the ambit of the global trading system were brought under the purview of WTO. They also included production and trade of agricultural produce, trade in services, intellectual property rights (IPRs), trade-related investment measures, etc. At the same time, quantitative trade barriers have been removed and tariff barriers have been decisively brought down. The export subsidies have also been brought down as they are regarded as trade distorting in nature. In addition, WTO has been empowered to establish a dispute settlement mechanism to sort out disputes among the trade partners called counteracting parties. The WTO has also been given authority to supervise implementation of GATT Agreements 1994 and punish the countries who do not fully comply with various provisions of the WTO (GATT Agreements 1994; 1995, Krueger, 1998). This institution is an open-ended organization which can bring in more issues for negotiation among the countries. The WTO is mandated with more authority to intervene in the global economy compared to any other multilateral institution such as the IMF and the World Bank. In a way, the formation of WTO has led to reduction in the sovereignty of the nation-state.

1.2 Globalization and State

In the post-colonial era, economies of countries have been organized under the nation-state. The nation-state has been a symbol and repository of sovereignty of a nation. The government is the ultimate source of authority and arbiter of dispute among its people. The role of nation-state increased in the advanced countries with the emergence of the welfare state. The state was engaged in management of effective demand to maintain full employment and provide several services to its citizens at concessional rates such as health, education, insurance, provision of public utilities, etc.

The state also managed in a harmonious way the relationship between capital and labour and created the image of cooperative capitalism. In the developing countries, the nation-state undertook development activities as a measure to catch up with the developed countries. The involvement of the state in economic activities ensured its entry into areas which were earlier left for private players. This created a situation for greater engagement of the nation-state in the economic and social activities of countries. This role got enhanced over time for nearly three decades after World War II. There was a tendency to give an internal orientation to economic nationalism by focusing on the internal market and welfare activities. This process reconciled to a large extent the economic nationalism of the individual nation-state with some degree of mutualism in international relations. The Cold War contributed to this process indirectly and the threat of socialism acted as a cementing factor to ideologically unite the capitalist market economies (Bhaduri, 2002; Hobsbawm, 1995). The nation-state achieved new heights in this era. There were variations in the degree of the role of the state in various countries— both developed and developing market economy countries— yet the direction was the same.

The new phase of globalization in the 1980s and 1990s has been accompanied by a gradual erosion of the role of the state. This process has resulted in a paradigm shift in development strategy from state-centric to market-centric. Globalization is accompanied by privatization of public enterprises and liberalization (freeing) of rules for private sector activities, making several operations of the nation-state redundant. Four factors have played a decisive role in this. First, the consolidation of MNCs in production (both goods and services) related activities as well as in the field of finance has made the closed economy-based nation-state model obsolete. These companies, with a huge amount of capital resources, technological leadership and highly skilled workforce, compel many nation-states to compromise their authority. In fact, they have evolved ways and means to bypass authority (rules) of the nation-state (Vernon, 1971). Second, international financial capital flows have eroded the authority of the state in fiscal and monetary managements. The financial flows at the global level have far exceeded the value of international trade and foreign investment. These financial flows move very quickly, with a destabilizing effect on the economy. Between 1977 and 1995, global foreign exchange turnover to the value of global exports rose from 3.5 to 64 and the official reserves declined from 15 days of daily foreign exchange turnover to less than that of a day (Felix, 1998). This has reduced considerably the capacity of governments to intervene in fiscal and monetary stabilization. Third, technological development, especially in communication technology, has increased the speed and efficiency of funds transfer manifold with implications for authority of state. It is not only the lightning speed with which funds are transferred but also the tremendous power of electronic media in shaping and influencing the sentiments that drive transactions in financial markets, that have serious constraints for the conduct of national macroeconomic policies (Bhaduri, 2002). Last, with the formation of the WTO from January 1, 1995, the nation-state has come to compromise its authority within the country. Earlier, in the area of agriculture, trade of agricultural produce, services, differential treatment of local and foreign companies, intellectual property rights, the nation-state could formulate policies and programmes autonomously. Now, such policies are subject to scrutiny of the WTO and the national policies have to be synchronized with the guidelines of the WTO. The countries that deviate from the guidelines face actions from the global agencies. The countries that approach international financial institutions in the wake of an internal economic crisis for financial assistance, have their policies constrained by conditions imposed by such agencies. This is especially the case with developing countries, which are borrowing under such circumstances from the IMF and the World Bank.

1.3 Globalization and Indian State

India introduced a major policy shift in June 1991 in the wake of the foreign exchange crisis it was facing. When Indian policy was in line with the Structural Adjustment Programme (SAP) of the World Bank, the latter extended the requisite financial support. India signed GATT Agreements 1994 and became a founder member of the WTO. These policy shifts have introduced far-reaching changes in the economy. Freedom has been given to companies for entry and exit through delicensing, removal of Monopolies and Restrictive Trade Practices (MRTP) Act and Foreign Exchange Regulation Act (FERA), many public sector enterprises have been privatized, public equity in many enterprises have been diluted; several areas, earlier reserved for the public sector, have been opened to the private sector, especially health, insurance, banking, infrastructure, roads, air transport, etc. The economy has been opened to the outside world both in trade of goods and services and for investment by foreign companies (MNC). There have been serious efforts by the government to adopt a policy of management of fiscal deficit by controlling public expenditure.

Faced with a financial crunch, both the union and state governments have made efforts to downsize themselves by stopping/postponement of fresh recruitments of employees. Amendments have been made in Indian patent laws to synchronize IPR regime to the WTO requirements. Electricity Bill 2003 has made it mandatory for states unbundle to State Electricity Boards (SEBs) is mandatory for the states. Private sector participation has been allowed in electricity, oil and natural gas, banking and insurance sectors, agricultural research and extension, medical health, and higher education. This has resulted a shrinkage in the role of government in running and management of the economy. The mainstream economists have produced a large volume of literature justifying the India's policy shift (Ahluwalia and Little, 1998; Joshi and Little, 1994 and 1996; Srinivasan, 2002). There are also some well-reasoned critiques of this policy trying to explain underlying processes and bringing out consequences for the people (Bhaduri and Nayyar, 1996; Nayyar 1995; Nayyar and Sen, 1994; Bhalla, 1994; Patnaik and Rawal, 2005). The discussion by scholars of different views brings out that the role of state has diminished over the reform period. The effort to give priority to fiscal management of the economy and withdrawal of the state from many areas has affected the capability of the Indian state and diminished its role in economic affairs. Its role has also changed from provider to facilitator in economic development. In economic planning, India has moved from physical planning to indicative planning (GOI, 1992).

1.4 Fiscal Distortions and Deceleration in Punjab

The economic prosperity in Punjab has been the direct outcome of the Green Revolution which appeared in the state in the mid-1960s. In fact, the Green Revolution itself materialized in Punjab due to the result of proactive state interventions in the economy through massive public investment channelled under two broad processes: technological inputs and institutional inputs. These inputs, in brief, include provision of high-yielding varieties of seeds, irrigation networking, cheap credit, machinery, fertilizers, tenancy reforms, assured purchase of produce, support prices, agricultural research and extension services, etc. The direct agricultural-oriented inputs along with the integrated programmes of rural development in the form of rural road connectivity, electrification, education and health services, and livestock and dairy development programmes kickstarted the on-farm and off-farm economic activities in the state. These policy instruments generated a propitious environment with strong focus on the agricultural and rural sectors that provided a big boost to the whole economy, including more public investments in social sectors of the state.

During the last four decades or so, the Punjab economy on the basis of economic growth in comparison to national average passed through three distinct phases: higher growth, equal growth, and lower growth. The economy of state grew at almost 7 per cent during the 1960s and 5.4 per cent during the 1970s, almost one-and-half to two times faster than that of the growth rate of national economy (World Bank, 2004). During the 1980s, Punjab's economic growth rate roughly matched that of the national average. In comparative terms, it was marginally lower during the Sixth Five Year Plan (1980–85) and marginally higher during the Seventh Five Year Plan (1985–90). But, during the whole decade of the1990s and thereafter, the state economy recorded a much lower growth rate than that of the national average. Indeed, it was 1.95 percentage points and 1.26 percentage points lower during the Eighth Five Year Plan (1992–97) and Ninth Five Year Plan (1997–2002) respectively. The same trend essentially persisted during the first three years (2002–03 to 2004–05) of the Tenth Five Year Plan (2002–07). Further, across the main sectors of Punjab's economy, the major slowdown in growth rate has been registered by the primary sector, particularly during the Ninth Five Year Plan (1997–2002), when the primary sector of state economy grew by just 1.84 per cent per annum as against the national average of 4.52 per cent per annum (Table 1.1). Thus, the state economy during the post-reforms period could not revert to its high trend growth rate that was realized during the pre-reforms period.

Table 1.1: Plan-Wise Real Growth Rate of Gross State Domestic Product: Punjab versus India (Annual Compound Growth Rates)

Plan Period	Primary	Secondary	Tertiary	Overall
1980–81 to 1984–85 (6th Plan) *	5.37 (5.63)	5.04 (6.05)	5.14 (5.42)	5.23 (5.66)
1985–86 to 1989–90 (7th Plan) *	5.24 (3.58)	8.65 (6.49)	5.22 (7.41)	5.98 (5.79)
1992–93 to 1996–97 (8th Plan) *	3.08 (3.85)	7.10 (8.28)	5.78 (7.77)	4.81 (6.76)
1997–98 to 2001–02 (9th Plan) **	1.84 (4.52)	6.20 (4.52)	5.38 (7.77)	4.08 (5.34)
(10th Plan) **				
2002–03	–3.50 (-5.61)	5.69 (6.35)	6.67 (7.91)	2.41 (3.98)
2003–04	6.23 (9.29)	4.56 (6.63)	7.43 (9.06)	6.29 (8.51)
2004–05	4.77 (n.a.)	4.57 (n.a.)	6.48 (n.a.)	5.39 (6.91)

* means at 1980–81 prices (for 1980–81 to 1996–97).

** means at 1993–94 prices (for 1997–98 to 2001–02).

Note: 1. Figures in parentheses represent India's growth rate.

2. Growth rates for Tenth Five Year Plan (2002 – 07) have been reported over the respective proceeding years.

Source: Statistical Abstract of Punjab, ESO, Chandigarh (various issues).

The economy of state has recorded noticeable changes in its production structure between 1980–81 and 2004–05 (Table 1.2). The share of the primary sector declined consistently and that of the tertiary sector increased in the Punjab economy. Within the primary sector, the major decline has occurred in the case of agriculture, viz. from 33.16 per cent in 1980–81 to 23.30 per cent during 2004–05. By comparing 2004–05 over 1990–91, all other sectors except the tertiary sector recorded a decline in their respective shares in state income. However, the employment structure (Table 1.3) in the state shows that, according to the Current Daily Status (CDS) criterion, the primary sector absorbed around 53 per cent of workforce during

1999–2000. Interestingly, this sector had experienced a major fall (11 percentage points) in its per cent share in the employment between 1983 (67.93 per cent) and 1993–94 (56.74 per cent), but witnessed a marginal fall (3.51 percentage points) in 1999–2000. So, two things are discernible and problematic, which, in fact, also indicates policy failures: First, the sizeable proportion of workforce in the state (53 per cent) were employed in primary sector whose share in the state income remained low (about 43 per cent); and second, between 1993–94 and 1999–2000 (post-reforms period), the annual rate of employment shifting from the primary sector to the most dynamic sectors of economy (secondary and tertiary sectors) has almost been halted. So, such intensification of structural rigidity in the employment market is reflected in the sphere of unemployment and poverty. The unemployment rate, i.e. proportion of workforce to labour force, measured on the CDS basis (open unemployment) was 2.6 per cent in rural areas and 3.2 per cent in urban areas during 1999–2000. Moreover, during the reforms period, its level has remained same in rural areas, but declined marginally in urban areas, i.e. 0.9 percentage points in about half a decade. Similarly, the poverty ratio recorded about six percentage points decline between 1993–94 and 1999–2000, but its level of about six per cent is quite high in a prosperous state.

The economic slowdown in the Punjab economy, which started during the 1980s and sharpened throughout the 1990s and beyond, has also been accompanied by the worsening of fiscal situation on the part of the state government. In fact, the state during the full decade of the 1980s extending up to the year 1992, witnessed militancy-based general turmoil on a large scale. This process has disturbed the state priorities from the developmental initiatives towards the law and order maintenance with a huge increase in the internal security apparatus, more public

Table 1.2: Percentage Distribution of Net State Domestic Product (NSDP) at Factor Cost in Punjab (Current Prices)

Sector	1980–81	1990–91	2000–01	2004–05 (Q)
1. Primary Sector	49.13	47.13	42.57	37.72
(a) Agriculture	33.16	31.25	27.28	23.30
(b) Live stock	14.44	15.23	14.65	13.92
2. Secondary Sector	20.01	24.38	21.49	22.27
3. Tertiary Sector	30.86	28.49	35.94	40.01
Total (1+2+3)	100.00	100.00	100.00	100.00

Source: Statistical Abstract of Punjab, ESO, Chandigarh (various issues).

Table 1.3: Employment Structure, Unemployment Rate and Poverty Levels in Punjab (Current Daily Status)

Major Head	1983	1993–94	1999–2000
1. Employment			
(a) Primary Sector	67.93	56.74	53.23
(b) Secondary Sector	12.75	15.63	17.51
(c) Tertiary Sector	19.32	27.62	29.26
Total (a+b+c)	100.00	100.00	100.00
2. Unemployment Rate			
Rural	–	2.7	2.6
Urban	–	4.1	3.2
3. Poverty Ratio	16.18	11.77	6.16

Source: (a) Government of India *(2002)*; (b) *Planning Commission (2003)*.

expenditure on security forces and their modernization and consequently more borrowings and debt on the state government, and hence shifting of spending priorities. Under the cumulative impact of decline in the budgetary support and lack of supervision and monitoring of the delivery mechanism, the effectiveness of public utilities reached its nadir. The democratic process in the state was restored in 1992 with the installation of an elected government and the state witnessed the end of militancy that very year. The subsequently elected democratic governments, instead of reorienting the state apparatus towards the development agenda, indulged in more popular election-oriented gimmicks (free electricity, free water, abolition of octroi, etc.), which played havoc with scarce state finances. During the 1990s, virtually no worthwhile attention was given to new means/methods to generate more resources for development purposes.

On the other side, the Indian economy entered the phase of economic reforms with the adoption of the New Economic Policy (1991) at the national-level. The state economy also followed the path of economic reforms under the adoption of NEP at the national-level. The whole policy package, in subsequent years till date, unfolded in a manner which resulted in complete by-passing of the social sectors, agricultural and rural economy, and other small and marginal producers and suppliers in other sectors of the economy. Moreover, the state could not attract any worthwhile level of Foreign Direct Investment (FDI) during the post-reforms period. For example, during August 1991 to March 2003, at the All-India level the total number of FDI approvals was 23,553, involving an investment of Rs. 2,85,525 crore. Out of these, the share of Punjab was 0.78 per cent (i.e. 185) in the approvals and 0.68 per cent (i.e. Rs. 1,968 crore) of total investment approved (EPW, 2003: 4499).

The agricultural sector in Punjab experienced deceleration because of decline in public investment. The subsidies in this area remained confined to mainly three inputs, viz. fertilizers, irrigation and electric power. The fertilizer subsidy was provided by the Centre and the rest two (irrigation and electric power) by the Punjab state. The total subsidy on these three inputs amounted to Rs. 932.8 crore in the triennium period ending 1990–91, Rs. 1,149.1 crore in the triennium period ending 1995–96, and Rs. 1,352.1 crores in the triennium period ending 2001–02 at the constant prices of 1993–94. These subsidies constituted respectively

7.7 per cent, 8.2 per cent, and 8.3 per cent of the Gross State Domestic Product (GSDP) produced in the agriculture sector of the state. Moreover, during the triennium ending 2001–02, the share of irrigation and power subsidies were 6 per cent and 71 per cent respectively (Vashishtha, 2005).

Table 1.4: Distribution of Public Expenditure by Major Heads in Punjab (Rs. in Crore at 1993–94 prices)

Triennium Period	Total Public Expenditure (All Heads)	Non-Development Expenditure	Development Expenditure		
			Economic Services	Social Services	Sub-Total
1978–79 to 1980–81	1520.24 (100.00)	410.71 (27.02)	483.80 (31.82)	625.73 (41.16)	1109.54 (72.98)
1981–82 to 1983–84	1889.60 (100.00)	571.45 (30.24)	576.17 (30.49)	741.97 (39.27)	1318.14 (69.76)
1984–85 to 1986–87	2383.50 (100.00)	837.89 (35.15)	613.46 (25.74)	932.16 (39.11)	1545.62 (64.85)
1987–88 to 1989–90	2994.60 (100.00)	955.39 (31.90)	708.72 (23.67)	1330.45 (44.43)	2039.17 (68.09)
1990–91 to 1992–93	4025.37 (100.00)	1365.99 (33.93)	1536.05 (38.16)	1153.73 (28.55)	2689.78 (66.70)
1993–94 to 1995–96	4686.01 (100.00)	2676.80 (57.12)	847.22 (18.08)	1161.97 (24.80)	2009.18 (42.88)
1996–97 to 1998–99	5537.74 (100.00)	2697.89 (48.72)	1363.16 (24.62)	1476.69 (26.67)	2839.84 (51.28)
1999–2000 to 2001–02	7044.19 (100.00)	4108.59 (58.33)	1155.10 (16.40)	1780.51 (25.28)	2935.60 (41.67)
2002–03 to 2004–05	9152.56 (100.00)	5395.67 (58.95)	1764.81 (19.28)	1992.08 (21.77)	3756.89 (41.05)

Note: Figures in parentheses are percentage shares.
Source: Statistical Abstract of Punjab, ESO, Chandigarh (various issues).

Since the public expenditures on the strategic social and economic services produce a large number of positive externalities in society, it would be interesting to examine the pattern of public expenditure on these services in the Punjab state. The analysis reveals that many significant shifts took place in the patterns of public expenditure in the state, particularly during the militancy-related political turmoil period of the 1980s and after the adoption of NEP-1991 during the period of 1990s and afterwards, which have negatively affected the delivery and monitoring mechanism of public services and socio-economic conditions of the poor people. The data on the pattern of public expenditure on revenue account in Punjab (Table 1.4) reveals that non-development expenditure at constant prices of 1993–94 spiralled from Rs. 410.71 crore per year (27.02 per cent) during the triennium period of 1978–79 to 1980–81, to Rs. 5,395.67 crore per year (58.95 per cent) during the triennium period of 2002–03 to 2004–05. And, the development expenditure increased from Rs.1,109.54 crore per year (72.98 per cent) to Rs. 3,756.89 crore per year (41.05 per cent) during the same period. Within the development expenditure in the state, allocation of funds in relative terms both to the economic services and social services has declined considerably during the given period. The expenditure on social services declined from 41.16 per cent (Rs. 625.73 crore per year) during the triennium period of 1978–79 to 1980–81 to 21.77 per cent (Rs. 1,992.08 crore per year) during the triennium period of 2002–03 to 2004–05. During the same period, the proportionate share of economic services also fell from 31.82 per cent (Rs. 483.80 crore per year) to 19.28 per cent (Rs. 1764.81crore per year). It means that non-development expenditure in the state has grown at a much faster rate than that of development expenditure.

The ever-rising non-development expenditure is largely attributed to the heavy state borrowings of the past; security-related mounting debt, burden of pensions and other miscellaneous expenditures. The data also support these views (Table 1.5) that expenditure on pension benefits of employees and miscellaneous services rose from Rs. 29.16 crore per year (7.10 per cent) during the triennium period of 1978–79 to 1980–81, Rs. 803.66 crore per year (30.02 per

Table 1.5: Distribution of Non-Development Public Expenditure by Major Components in Punjab

(Figures in Rs. Crore at 1993–94 prices)

	Major Constituents of Non-Development Expenditure						
Triennium Period	**Organs of State**	**Fiscal Services**	**Interest Payments and Debt Services**	**General Administration Services**	**Pensions and Miscellaneous Services**	**Other Grants-in-Aid**	**Total Non-Development Expenditure**
1978–79 to1980–81	17.73 (4.32)	25.08 (6.11)	173.21 (42.17)	161.48 (39.32)	29.16 (7.10)	4.05 (0.98)	410.71 (100.00)
1981–82 to1983–84	19.04 (3.33)	31.05 (5.43)	229.94 (40.24)	218.63 (38.26)	67.66 (11.84)	5.14 (0.90)	571.45 (100.00)
1984–85 to1986–87	22.40 (2.67)	34.19 (4.08)	349.58 (41.72)	280.86 (33.52)	125.62 (14.99)	25.24 (3.01)	837.89 (100.00)
1987–88 to1989–90	28.38 (2.97)	44.13 (4.62)	343.14 (35.92)	381.64 (39.95)	129.22 (13.53)	28.87 (3.02)	955.39 (100.00)
1990–91 to1992–93	32.39 (2.37)	46.44 (3.40)	451.17 (33.03)	619.75 (45.37)	178.32 (13.05)	37.91 (2.78)	1365.99 (100.00)
1993–94 to1995–96	42.21 (1.58)	63.56 (2.37)	1142.45 (42.68)	573.35 (21.42)	803.66 (30.02)	51.58 (1.93)	2676.80 (100.00)
1996–97 to1998–99	60.63 (2.25)	77.14 (2.86)	1404.19 (52.05)	686.92 (25.46)	417.76 (15.48)	51.25 (1.90)	2697.89 (100.00)
1999–00 to2001–02	64.82 (1.58)	92.34 (2.25)	1679.85 (40.89)	721.19 (17.55)	1488.29 (36.22)	62.10 (1.51)	4108.59 (100.00)
2002–03 to2004–05	79.62 (1.48)	104.52 (1.94)	2070.91 (38.38)	854.75 (15.84)	2200.86 (40.79)	85.01 (1.58)	5395.67 (100.00)

Note: Figures in parentheses are percentage shares.
Source: Statistical Abstract of Punjab, ESO, Chandigarh (various issues).

cent) during the triennium period of 1993–94 to 1995–96, and Rs. 2,200.86 crore per year (40.79 per cent) during the triennium period of 2002–03 to 2004–05. Expenditure on interest payments and debt services of the state increased from Rs. 173.21 crore per year (42.17 per cent) during the triennium period of 1978–79 to 1980–81 and Rs. 1,404.19 crore per year (52.05 per cent) during the triennium period of 1996–97 to 1998–99. After that, the absolute amount of expenditure on this head rose to Rs. 1,679.85 crore per year (40.89 per cent) during the triennium period of 1999–2000 to 2001–02, and 2,070.91 crore per year (38.38 per cent) during the triennium period of 2002–03 to 2004–05. General administrative services, which had attracted about two-fifth of total non-development expenditure (40 per cent) up to the triennium period ending in 1992–93, declined its share to 15.84 per cent (Rs. 854.75 crore per year) during the triennium period of 2002–03 to 2004–05. Although the expenditures on state organs and fiscal services have mounted up in absolute terms, the proportionate share of these services has declined over the time period of study. Thus, the ever-rising non-development expenditure is not a healthy sign for Punjab's future developmental process and actually diminishes its growth potentials.

In the light of the above discussion, it is useful to make a sector-specific study of the role of government/state in India. The present study is largely concentrated on the service sector, especially health, education and agricultural extension. These are the areas in which the (state) government plays a decisive role due to Constitutional obligations and specific requirements of the society. These are the areas where the continuation of the role of state/government is not questioned by institutions like the WTO. These areas have been opened up to private sector activities in the country. Consequently, under the WTO guidelines, the foreign service providers have to be allowed and given equal treatment. The entry of private players (both Indian and foreign) have many implications. They are related, on the one side, to the high prices/costs of these services which may be beyond the affordable reach of the common consumers. On the other side, this raises issues related to service conditions of the workforce engaged in providing these services. At the same time, the affordability, quality and efficiency of these services to the disadvantaged group of persons and to the disadvantaged areas are of permanent importance. These services have to be provided efficiently to everyone to meet his/her requirements.

Therefore, the issues of access, affordability and quality of these services merit attention in the policy debates. Recognizing the importance of these issues, in some services (especially electricity and telecommunication), the government created a regulatory mechanism.* The present study is focused on the delivery of education, health and agriculture extension services in the state of Punjab. In the education sector, the main emphasis is on primary education, while in the health services, the emphasis has been on primary as well as secondary healthcare. The agricultural extension has no layers except for different types of service providers. Therefore, agricultural extension services have been evaluated as a whole.

1.5 Objectives of the Study

The study is intended to achieve the following specific objectives:

1. to examine the various dimensions of the budgetary spending in the state of Punjab;
2. to examine the mode of public delivery of health,

* However, no regulatory authority has been established to monitor and regulate the entry of private players in the areas of health, education and agriculture extension services.

education and agricultural extension services;
3. to examine the changes in the mode of delivery of these services in the post-reforms period;
4. to examine the comparative supply of public resources for these services during the pre and post-reforms period;
5. to bring out factors behind improvement/deterioration of delivery of these services;
6. to measure the impact of entry of new players on public delivery of these services and make comparative analysis; and
7. to make policy suggestions for improvement in delivery system of these services.

1.6 Scope of the Study

The study is intended to evaluate delivery of education, health and agriculture extension services in Punjab. Punjab, being agriculturally one of the most developed states, has been chosen purposely. In this state, significant changes in the pattern of delivery system of these services have been experimented in the post-reforms period. In the area of health, the government created Punjab Health Systems Corporation (PHSC) after it was provided a major loan by the World Bank to improve the delivery of public health services in the state. In the area of education, a whole range of private institutions has been allowed from the primary to higher education system. In the area of agriculture extension, Government of Punjab has allowed several private companies in contract farming with the provision that the companies would provide extension services to farmers entering into contract with them and would charge for the services. It would be extremely useful to examine the system and conceptualization of delivery of these services in Punjab. Since Punjab has ventured into several experiments in these areas (compared to other provinces in the region), this makes the study relevant and topical. The location of present researchers in this state and intimate involvement in public discussions provide an additional advantage in the selection of Punjab as the study area. The study covers the post-reforms period from 1991 to 2005. However, an attempt has also been made to understand the situation in a comparative framework by examining the quantum and flow of public resources during the pre and post-reforms period.

1.7 Data and Methodology

The study is largely based on secondary data collected from various government departments by establishing contact with concerned officials. The statistical reports issued by the government agencies form the basis of the study. The information gaps have been filled through the primary data. For this purpose, appropriate sample design has been developed and data collected through questionnaires. The work of scholars who have worked in these areas has also been consulted. Attempt has been made to quantify the efficiency level by using some vital variables as indicators of performance. The policy documents of government have also been consulted and personal interviews have been sought from policy makers/government officials for discussion on related issues.

The period of study has been quite long, spanning 1978–79 to 2004–05. Depending upon the availability of data, it has also been adjusted. In the case of the education, particularly about the flow of the public resources to this sector, the period has been compressed and ended in 2001–02. The important thing is that the general framework of the study followed in case of all of the issues remained the same. The flow of resources has been examined in the pre and post-reforms period, i.e. is from 1978–79 to 1989–90 and 1990–91 to 2001–02. The growth rates have been examined in real prices also by using the Net State Domestic Product (NSDP) deflators at 1993–94 prices. In order to highlight the priorities in the spending by the state, the share of public expenditures on various services has been examined in relation to state budget and state income. The real price growth of the various variables during the period throw much light on the relative priority and general resource situation of that sector. The distribution of the public expenditure among the various sub sectors of the particular sector has also been analyzed in order to understand the spending priorities among the various sectors. The performance of the various sectors has been examined by using the appropriate output indicators. To further decipher the inter-period changes and trends, the data over the various Plan periods have also been viewed. The participation and access to various services has also been viewed from the angle of different types of users spread across various socio-economic and spatial layers. The state role has also been assessed by taking into account the number of vacancies filled and vacant posts pertaining to these public utilities. Thus, the study presents in a comprehensive framework the real situation of various sectors during the process of globalization.

1.8 Chapter Scheme

The study is divided into following chapters:

1. Introduction
2. Education Sector in Punjab
3. Health Services in Punjab
4. Agriculture Extension Services in Punjab
5. Summary, Conclusions and Policy Recommendations.

2

The Education Sector in Punjab

The development-oriented research demonstrates that education contributes to growth and development by immense amounts and in multifarious ways. And, education is also considered the single largest determinant of socio-economic transformation. Moreover, education affects the inner core of economic activities both in the market and household spheres. Further, educational investment is more productive and enduring, and it generates a return more than any other form of physical investment (Todaro, 1985; Meier and Rauch, 2000). Furthermore, the build up of basic education generates a high component of externality by influencing the general fertility, and infant, child and maternal mortality along with nutritional status of populace (World Bank, 1997). In this way, the presence of social benefits makes education the classic case of public good and thereby contains a strong rationale for its public subsidization (Tilak, 2004).

The discovery and ultimate realization of growth enhancing values of education led to the involvement of public resources in the education sector. This involvement acquired either the form of direct public provisioning of the supply of educational services or through providing of public subsidies to the private suppliers, or some mixture of both of the methods. However, the degree and manner of the involvement of public resources vary across the countries and within the countries across the various regions and provinces. In advanced countries, there has been tremendous involvement of public resources in the education sector. For example, the USA and UK each had spent as much as 5.4 per cent of their respective national income on education through public resources (HDR, 1999). Thereby, the per-capita public spending on education was $1,394 in 1996 in the USA (Mittar, Singh and Brar, 2002: 40). The massive involvement of public resources in education resulted in the substantial improvement in the mean years of schooling in the advanced countries. However, in the developing world, in general, the education sector has been facing a resource crunch and has been the victim of low level of priority by the successive political regimes (Dreze and Sen, 1995). The problem got further aggravated with the adoption of the new economic policy regime which paved the way for commercialization of education, and it has turned education from being a social service to a marketable commodity to be supplied at cost plus basis depending upon the market structure for its particular level and variety. It is noticeable that the process of structural adjustment affects the course of any sector by its macro-economic impacts and micro-economic linkages. The evidence of reduction in public expenditure on education during adjustment phase was pervasive (Noss, 1991). Further, the decline of public expenditure on education in a situation of greater income inequality and imposition of user charges poses the real danger of pricing out of weaker sections from availing of such service (Upendranadh, 1993). The problem becomes further complicated because the so-called free education in the country is not truly free as it involves many charges besides tuition fee (Tilak, 1996).

2.1 Existing Scenario

Punjab state's education structure, particularly the school education, is based on the national pattern of 12 years (10+2) of schooling. The school education consists of eight years of compulsory elementary education (I–VIII) consisting of the primary education (I–V) and the middle education (VI–VIII) levels, two years of high/secondary education (IX–X) and two years of senior secondary education (XI–XII). Besides this, it has two/three years of pre-primary education, mostly prevalent in the aided and/or unaided schools. After high school or senior secondary education level, some students join the Industrial Training Institutes (ITIs), Polytechnics, etc. to acquire low-level skills. Recently, the Punjab government has merged the primary education (I–V) and the middle education (VI–VIII) levels into the elementary education to synchronize it with the national level by forming an elementary directorate.

2.1.1 Growing Number of Schools

In Punjab, school education has been imparted through a well-defined institutional framework consisting of the primary schools, middle schools and high/higher or senior secondary schools established by the state sector and the private sector. There were 12,384 primary schools, 1,410 middle schools and 2,419 high/higher secondary schools in 1981 (Table 2.1). Their number rose to 13,352 for primary schools, 2,503 middle schools and 3,980 high/higher secondary schools in 2004. The data reveal that, between 1981 and 2004, opening of new primary schools slowed down to the minimum level (968 schools in 24 years), whereas between 1971 and 1981, 6013 new primary schools were established in Punjab (Mittar, Singh and Brar, 2002). On the other hand, only 81 and 887 primary schools were added in Punjab during the periods 1981–91 and 1991–2004 respectively. The compound growth rate in primary schools between 1981 and 2004 worked out to be very low, i.e. 0.76 per cent per annum (Table 2.2). Among primary schools, the compound growth rate was found to be higher in the urban areas (4.51 per cent per annum) than in the rural areas (0.36 per cent per annum).

Table 2.1: Government and Non-Government Schools (Recognized) in Punjab by Education Level, 1981–2004

Education Level		1981	1991	2004
Primary (I–V)	R	11,396 [70.29] (92.02)	11,361 [68.24] (91.14)	11,816 [59.57] (88.50)
	U	988 [6.09] (7.98)	1,104 [6.63] (8.86)	1,536 [7.74] (11.50)
	T	12,384 [76.38] (100.00)	12,465 [74.87] (100.00)	13,352 [67.32] (100.00)
Middle (VI–VIII)	R	1286 [7.93] (91.21)	1208 [7.26] (85.07)	2277 [11.48] (90.97)
	U	124 [0.76] (8.79)	212 [1.27] (14.93)	226 [1.14] (9.03)
	T	1,410 [8.69] (100.00)	1,420 [8.53] (100.00)	2,503 [12.62] (100)
High/Higher or Senior Secondary (IX–XII)	R	1,768 [10.90] (73.09)	2,057 [12.36] (74.42)	2,936 [14.80] (73.77)
	U	651 [4.02] (26.91)	707 [4.24] (25.58)	1,044 [5.26] (26.23)
	T	2,419 [14.92] (100.00)	2,764[16.60] (100.00)	3,980 [20.07] (100)
Total	R	14,450[89.13] (89.13)	14,626 [87.85] (87.85)	17,029 [85.85] (85.85)
	U	1,763[10.87] (10.87)	2,023 [12.15] (12.15)	2,806 [14.15] (14.15)
	T	16,213 [100.00] (100.00)	16,649 [100.00] (100.00)	19,835 [100] (100.00)

Note: (a) R = Rural, U = Urban, T = Total
(b) Figures in parentheses (...) are percentages and in index brackets [...] are percentage share of the total.

Source: 1. *Social and Educational Statistics of Punjab*, ESO, Chandigarh (various issues).
2. *Statistical Abstract of Punjab 2002*, ESO, Chandigarh (various issues).
3. *Economic Survey of Punjab*, ESO, Chandigarh (various issues).

The number of middle schools increased from 1,410 in 1981 to 1,420 in 1991 and 2,503 in 2004; and that of high/higher or senior secondary schools from 2,419 in 1981 to 2,764 in 1991 and to 3,980 in 2004. They grew at the rate of 1.34 per cent per annum during 1981–1991 and 3.71 per cent per annum during 1991–2004. Further, compound growth

Table 2.2: Growth of Government and Non-Government Schools (Recognized) in Punjab by Education Level, 1981–2004.

Education Level		Compound Growth Rate Per Annum		
		1981–2004	**1981–1991**	**1991–2004**
Primary (I–V)	R	0.36	–0.03	0.39
	U	4.51	1.12	3.36
	T	0.76	0.06	0.69
Middle (VI–VIII)	R	5.88	–0.62	6.54
	U	6.19	5.51	0.64
	T	5.91	0.07	5.84
High/Higher or Senior Secondary (IX–XII)	R	5.20	1.53	3.62
	U	4.84	0.83	3.97
	T	5.11	1.34	3.71
Total	R	1.66	0.12	1.53
	U	4.76	1.39	3.33
	T	2.04	0.27	1.77

Note: R = Rural, U = Urban, T = Total

Source: 1. *Social and Educational Statistics of Punjab*, ESO, Chandigarh (various issues).
2. *Statistical Abstract of Punjab 2002*, ESO, Chandigarh (various issues).
3. *Economic Survey of Punjab*, ESO, Chandigarh (various issues).

rates among the middle schools located in rural and urban areas do not show many variations. However, in the case of high/higher or senior secondary schools, rural schools grew at the growth rate of 5.20 per cent per annum as compared to the growth rate of 5.11 per cent per annum among urban schools between 1981 and 2004. The deceleration in the growth rate of the primary schools compared to the growth rate of middle schools and high/higher or senior secondary schools in Punjab indicates that this is largely due to the large-scale upgradation of the existing primary schools to the higher level of education in the state.

The location-wise information of schools points out that, in Punjab, about 90 per cent of the primary and the middle schools are located in rural areas. Similarly, about three-fourth majority of high/higher or senior secondary schools are located in rural Punjab. Their proportion, however, has increased marginally from 73.09 per cent in 1981 to 73.77 per cent in 2004. Thus, education facilities at the school level are fairly adequate in rural Punjab as the number and proportion of rurally located schools are much higher than that of the share of rural population (65.05 per cent as per 2001 Census). Thus, rural-urban distribution of schools in Punjab seems to be rational.

2.1.2 Management Pattern of Schools

Another striking feature of growth of schools in Punjab is related to the significant role played by the state in expanding access to education between 1981 and 2001 by opening new/upgrading old schools, particularly at the high/higher or senior secondary education level. On the other hand, non-government schools have also gained importance in the state's education sector during the same period. It would, therefore, be more interesting to analyze the growth of government-owned and non-government owned (aided and non-aided) schools in Punjab. Table 2.3 reveals the distribution of schools on the basis of ownership status. The analysis of data shows that, on the whole, there were 15,473 government schools in Punjab in 1981 and their number rose to 15,658 in 1991(185 new schools added during 1981–1991) and 17,656 schools in 2001(1,998 new schools were added during 1991– 2001). The government owned schools, however, have grown at the compound growth rate of 0.66 per cent per annum only between 1981 and 2001; 0.12 per cent per annum between 1981 and1991, and 1.21 per cent per annum between 1991 and 2001. On the other hand, the number of non-government schools have increased from 740 schools (4.57 per cent) in 1981 to 991 (5.45 per cent) in 1991 and to 1,832 (9.40 per cent) in 2001. Among the non-government schools, the compound growth rate worked out to be 4.64 per cent per annum between 1981and 2001; 2.96 per cent per annum between 1981 and 1991, and 6.35 per cent per annum between 1991 and 2001 (Table 2.4). Thus, compound growth rate among the non-government schools is much higher than that of the government schools during all the time periods.

Table 2.3: Distribution of Recognized Schools in Punjab by Type of Management and Education Level, 1981–2001

Education Level		**Number of Schools**		
		1981	**1991**	**2001**
Primary	Government	12,227 (98.57)	12,162 (97.57)	12,176 (93.12)
	Non-Government	157 (1.27)	303 (2.43)	900 (6.88)
	Total	12,384 (100.00)	12,465 (100.00)	13,076 (100.00)
Middle	Government	1,325 (93.97)	1,293 (91.06)	2,357 (93.83)
	Non-Government	85 (6.03)	127 (8.94)	155 (6.17)
	Total	1,410 (100.00)	1,420 (100.00)	2,512 (100.00)
High/Higher or Senior Secondary	Government	1,921 (79.41)	2,203 (79.70)	3,123 (80.08)
	Non-Government	498 (20.59)	561 (20.29)	777 (19.92)
	Total	2,419 (100.00)	2,764 (100.00)	3,900 (100.00)
Total	Government	15,473 (95.43)	15,658 (94.05)	17,656 (90.60)
	Non-Government	740 (4.57)	991 (5.95)	1,832 (9.40)
	Total	16,213 (100.00)	16,649 (100.00)	19,488 (100.00)

Note: 1. Government schools include schools owned by the state and union governments (including local bodies). Non-government schools comprise aided/non-aided private schools.
2. Figures in brackets are percentages.

Source: 1. As reported in Table 2.1.
2. Office of DPI (Schools), Government of Punjab, Chandigarh.

Table 2.4: Growth of Recognized Schools in Punjab by Type of Management and Education Level, 1981–2001 (Per cent)

Education Level		Compound growth rate per annum		
		1981–2001	1981–1991	1991–2001
Primary	Government	–0.02	–0.05	0.01
	Non-Government	9.12	6.80	11.50
	Total	0.27	0.06	0.48
Middle	Government	2.92	–0.24	6.19
	Non-Government	3.08	4.09	2.08
	Total	2.93	0.07	5.87
High/Higher or Senior Secondary	Government	2.46	1.38	3.55
	Non-Government	2.26	1.20	3.32
	Total	2.42	1.34	3.51
Total	Government	0.66	0.12	1.21
	Non-Government	4.64	2.96	6.35
	Total	0.92	0.27	1.59

Note: 1. Government schools include schools owned by the state and union governments (including local bodies). Non-government schools comprise of aided/non-aided private schools.
2. Figures in brackets are percentages.

Source: 1. As reported in Table 2.1.
2. Office of DPI (Schools), Government of Punjab, Chandigarh.

At the primary level, the number as well as the proportion of government-owned schools decreased from 98.57 per cent (12,227 schools) in 1981 to 97.57 per cent (12,162 schools) in 1981 and then marginally rose to 93.12 per cent (12,176 schools) in 2001. The number of non-government primary schools increased from 157 schools (1.27 per cent) in 1981 to 303 schools (2.43 per cent) in 1991 and 900 schools (6.88 per cent) in 2001. The compound growth rate among government primary schools during 1981–2001 declined at the rate of –0.02 per cent per annum compared to the growth rate of 9.12 per cent per annum among non-government primary schools. Among the middle schools, the proportion of government school decreased from 93.83 per cent (1325 schools) in 1981 to 91.06

per cent (1293 schools) in 1991, and rose to 93.97 per cent (2357 schools) in 2001. The compound growth rate of 3.08 per cent per annum among the non-government middle schools has been found to be higher than that of government-owned middle schools (2.92 per cent per annum). In the case of high/higher or senior secondary schools, the proportion of non-government schools has remained constant at around one-fifth of schools between 1981 and 2001, despite an increase in their absolute numbers. The compound growth rate in the case of government-owned high/higher or senior secondary schools has been higher compared to the growth rate of non-government schools during all the time periods of study.

Interestingly, across the different levels of education, the proportionate share of non-government high/higher or senior secondary schools has been found to be very high (19.92 per cent) compared to the non-government primary schools (6.88 per cent) and middle schools (6.17 per cent) in 2001. In Punjab, at present, the government manages an overwhelming majority of all the recognized school education institutions. However, a growing number of non-government schools at all education levels, with official recognition, and in many cases, with financial assistance of state government, has been found. Non-government schools are, therefore, entering the education sector in a big way.

In the last decade or so, there has been a rapid growth in the number of unrecognized privately financed primary schools in Punjab. These schools have begun to attract an increasing proportion of total number of students. For instance, the proportion of students enrolled in these unrecognized private schools at the primary level reached 24.50 per cent in 2000–01 from 20.34 per cent in 1995–96 (Table 2.5). On the other hand, the share of students enrolled in government-owned primary schools (I–V classes)

Table 2.5: Percentage Distribution of Students Enrolled at Primary Level in Punjab by School Recognition Pattern.

Year	Government Schools	Recognized Schools	Unrecognized Schools	Total
1995–96	71.66	8.00	20.34	100.00
1996–97	71.86	8.90	19.24	100.00
1997–98	70.68	9.03	20.29	100.00
1998–99	70.91	8.87	20.22	100.00
1999–2000	69.48	8.40	22.12	100.00
2000–2001	66.28	9.22	24.50	100.00

Source: Office of DPI (Schools), Government of Punjab, Chandigarh.

gradually declined to 66.28 per cent in 2000–01 from 71.66 per cent in 1995–96. The proportionate share of students enrolled in the recognized non-government primary schools went up to 9.22 per cent from 8.00 per cent during the same period.

This larger growth in the proportion of students' enrolment in these unrecognized primary schools reflects the diminishing confidence of the people in government-managed schools. These government schools not only lack basic infrastructural facilities, they are also bereft of motivation and commitment among the teachers they employ. Hence, households having higher income and educational levels prefer to admit their children in private schools, whereas they (parents) seem to perceive that their child would be imparted qualitatively better education. The state government must follow, without undermining their role in enrolling students who might otherwise be out of schools, the liberal but strict public policy to enlist these unrecognized schools so that these could be brought under some kind of checks and controls, and also enable the state to find the 'missing but prized students' not included in the educational database of the state.

After the family, school is, indeed, considered to be one of the main agencies of learning process and socialization of a child. Arguably, the first prerequisite of schooling is availability of good quality and attractive infrastructure in each school for imparting education. Hence, a school must be attractive in terms of its environment. However, the data in Table 2.6 do not reveal a very positive picture of the infrastructural facilities available in the schools of Punjab. On the whole, there are 1,153 schools (6.18 per cent) without their own buildings, 6,761 schools (36.23 per cent) without a boundary wall, 7,976 schools (42.74 per cent) without the playgrounds and 13,179 schools (70.62 per cent) without the facility of toilets for children. Although lack of infrastructural facilities such as buildings, playgrounds, toilets, etc. is more pronounced in the primary and middle schools, there are many high and senior secondary schools

Table 2.6: Number of Schools Lacking Infrastructural Facilities in Punjab by School Level, 1999.

	Schools Lacking Infrastructural Facility					
School Level	**Buildings**	**Verandas**	**Boundary Walls**	**Play-grounds**	**Toilets**	**Total Schools**
Primary	676 (4.91)	3,780 (27.45)	4,995 (36.28)	6,147 (44.64)	10,770 (78.22)	13,769
Middle	303 (12.97)	1,107 (47.39)	1,120 (47.95)	1,140 (48.80)	1,552 (66.44)	2,336
High	138 (7.99)	545 (31.54)	480 (27.78)	508 (29.40)	640 (37.04)	1,728
Senior Secondary	36 (4.34)	186 (22.44)	166 (20.02)	181 (21.83)	217 (26.18)	829
Total	1,153 (6.18)	5,618 (30.10)	6,761 (36.23)	7,976 (42.74)	13,179 (70.62)	18,662

Note: 1. Total number of schools also includes the functional schools.
2. Figures in parentheses are percentage shares to the respective total schools.

Source: *Office of DPI (School)*, Government of Punjab, Chandigarh.

also bereft of these facilities. About 8 per cent of high schools did not have their own buildings, 27.28 per cent require boundary walls, 29.40 per cent playgrounds and 37.04 per cent toilets. Similarly, at the senior secondary education level, 4.34 per cent schools are without own buildings, 20.02 per cent have no boundary walls, 21.83 per cent lack playgrounds and 26.18 per cent are without toilets. Interestingly, at the senior secondary level where the children are grownup and need to have privacy, there are no proper separate toilets for girls in a sufficiently large number of schools.

Further, the information collected by the Directorate of School Education in Punjab too reveals that 60 per cent of the primary schools and 58 per cent of the middle schools require additional classrooms. Moreover, 69 per cent of the high and 73 per cent of the senior secondary schools too are facing a shortage of classrooms, despite a programme for the construction of more classrooms, to the extent these were deficient, being declared as a major target in the National Policy on Education 1986. The estimated numbers of additional classrooms required are 18,002 at the primary level, 4,150 at the middle level, 4,091 at the high and 3,239 at the senior secondary level. Besides, there are also shortage of such basic necessities in the schools as chalks, dusters and blackboards, what to speak of furniture, i.e. desk, bench, chair or even a mat for rural students. The data speak volumes about the worst state of infrastructure in government schools in Punjab (Planning Commission, 2003).

Apart from the shortage of physical inputs, there are many glaring deficiencies in Punjab's school education that have adversely affected both the quality of education and the creativity of students. Important deficiencies among these are: heavy prescribed syllabi, outdated teaching practices, decreased motivation and commitment among teachers, poor governance and supervisory mechanism, absenteeism among rurally posted teachers, shortage of teachers, low income and education levels of parents, etc. The present mode of school teaching/learning is a matter of great concern when one view that more than 90 per cent of children of the primary school age group (6–11 years) have ever been admitted to recognize primary schools, and only 58 per cent appear for the matriculation examination in the state.

2.1.3 Students' Enrolment and Teachers

The constrained supply of public resources and unregulated entry and functioning of private players has serious implications in terms of educational participation and outcomes. The total number of students in the elementary stage declined from 29.93 lakh (1991) to 29.43 lakh (2004) (Table 2.7). Noticeably, their number increased in absolute sense in 1991 (29.93 lakh) over 1981 (27.10 lakh). Further, in secondary education, though the number of students improved between 1991 and 2004, compared with the first period the addition was of small magnitude. Moreover, the number of students in schools increased by 1.92 lakh in 2004 over that of 1991, whereas the addition was 5.91 lakh in 1991 over 1981. The data also show that the number and proportion of students belonging to Scheduled Castes improved. Interestingly, their proportion (39.57 per cent) in overall has gone up more than that of their share in population of the state, i.e. 28.90 per cent in 2001. In this context, it is to be noted that this has been the outcome of shifting of their wards, by those parents who could afford good private education, from the government schools in favour of the private ones.

As another consequence of resource constraint, the absolute number of teachers has declined during 2004 from

Table 2.7: Enrolment of Students, Overall and Scheduled Castes, in Punjab by Education Level and Sex (1981–2004) (Number of Students in Lakh)

Level		1981	1991	2004
Elementary (1–VIII)	B	15.29 [28.78] (56.42)	16.32 [32.60] (54.53)	15.65 [43.19] (53.18)
	G	11.81 [25.15] (43.58)	13.61 [29.98] (45.47)	13.78 [44.27] (46.82)
	T	27.10 [27.20] (100)	29.93 [31.41] (100)	29.43 [43.70] (100)
Secondary (IX–XII)	B	1.88 [18.62] (62.05)	3.54 [20.34] (57.94)	4.58 [25.41] (53.59)
	G	1.15 [11.30] (37.95)	2.57 [16.73] (42.06)	3.95 [21.85] (46.31)
	T	3.03 [15.84] (100)	6.11 [18.82] (100)	8.53 [25.31] (100)
Total	B	17.17 [27.66] (56.99)	19.86 [30.41] (55.11)	20.23 [39.13] (53.29)
	G	12.96 [23.92] (43.01)	16.18 [27.87] (44.89)	17.73 [40.07] (46.71)
	T	30.13 [26.05] (100)	36.04 [29.27] (100)	37.96 [39.57] (100)

Note: 1. Percentage shares of Scheduled Caste students are given in squared brackets.
2. B for Boys, G for Girls, and T for Total.

Source: 1. *Social and Educational Statistics of Punjab*, ESO, Chandigarh (various issues).
2. *Statistical Abstract of Punjab*, ESO, Chandigarh (various issues).
3. *Economic Survey of Punjab*, ESO, Chandigarh (various issues).

their number during 1991 (Table 2.8). In the earlier period, their number had improved in 1991 over 1981. Further, the number of teachers has improved at the secondary level of education during the reform period. But, the proportion of elementary-level teachers declined among the total number of school teachers. With such an interplay of the number of students and teachers, the pupil-teacher ratio at elementary level of education deteriorated from 35.63 (1991) to 35.99 (2004). It improved marginally at the secondary level of education from 25.29 (1991) to 23.61 (2004).

Table 2.8: Number of Teachers, and Pupil-Teacher Ratio, 1981–2004

Level of Education	1981	1991	2004
Elementary (1–VIII)	78,737 [34.42] (81.17)	84,014 [35.63] (77.67)	81,770 [35.99] (69.35)
Secondary (IX–XII)	18,266 [16.59] (18.83)	24,158 [25.29] (22.33)	36,131 [23.61] (30.65)
Total	97,003 [31.06] (100)	108,172 [33.32] (100)	117,901 [32.20] (100)

Note: 1. Figures in round parentheses are percentage share of the total.
2. The figures in square parentheses are pupil-teacher ratios.

Source: 1. *Social and Educational Statistics of Punjab*, ESO, Chandigarh (various issues).
2. *Statistical Abstract of Punjab*, ESO, Chandigarh (various issues).
3. *Economic Survey of Punjab*, ESO, Chandigarh (various issues).

2.1.4 Literacy and Enrolment Ratio

The state has experienced significant change in the scenario pertaining to literacy. Literacy as such is a weak indicator of human capital formation and in its measurement the quality of education gets ignored. In the country, a person is counted as literate in the census enumeration if one can read and write with understanding in any language. However, it is to be noted that the literacy rate has a strong connection with educational progress, which comes from schooling. So, schooling leads to a change in literacy level among all sections of society. The overall literacy rate (Table 2.9) in the state increased from 48.10 per cent in 1981, to 58.51 per cent in 1991, and to 69.95 per cent in 2001. But, in 2001, about 30 per cent of the population in the literacy-eligible-category (six years and above) was illiterate. During the period of two decades (i.e. 1981 to 2001), the literacy rate recorded 1.89 per cent annual compound growth rate. Moreover, the growth in literacy rate slowed down during the decade of 1991–2001 (i.e. 1.77 per cent) than that of the decade of 1981–1991 (i.e. 1.98 per cent). It seems that until and unless adequate measures are taken, it would take a

Table 2.9: Indian Punjab: Literacy Levels and Change

Group	1981	1991	2001	Annual Compound Growth Rate		
				1981–91	1991–01	1981–2001
(a) Overall	48.10	58.51	69.95	1.98	1.77	1.89
(b) Male	55.53	65.66	75.63	1.69	1.40	1.56
(c) Female	39.60	50.41	63.55	2.44	2.29	2.39
Gap (b-c)	15.93	15.25	12.08			
(d) Rural	35.20	52.77	64.70	4.13	2.02	3.09
(e) Urban	55.63	72.08	79.10	2.62	0.93	1.78
Gap (d-e)	20.43	19.31	14.40			

Note: Literacy rates are for seven years and above.
Source: *Statistical Abstract of Punjab*, ESO, Chandigarh, (various issues).

considerable number of years for the state to eradicate illiteracy.

Further, the educational progress in the state is highly iniquitous in terms of regions, districts, locations, sexes and population groups. The male literacy in 2001 was 75.63 per cent and female 63.55 per cent. The urban literacy stood at 79.10 per cent and rural literacy at 64.70 per cent in 2001. Interestingly, in all literacy categories, the growth rate declined in the 1990s as compared to the1980s. But, on the other side, the gap in the literacy rates between males and females and those of between rural and urban categories, slightly narrowed down. During the decade of the1980s, the gap declined just marginally between sexes and locations. And, during the1990s, the gap declined a little more, i.e. 3.17 percentage point sex-wise and 4.91 percentage points location-wise. Thus, the literacy gaps would persist in the state in view of the slower pace of literacy improvement.

An assessment of gross enrolment rates in Punjab (Table 2.10) reveals some interesting points. *One*, gross enrolment rate at the primary level for boys has increased from 79.48 per cent in 1971 to 97.80 per cent in 1981. The

Table 2.10: Gross Enrolment Ratio in Punjab by Gender and Education Level

Education Level	Sex	1981	1991	2000
Primary(I–V)	Boys	97.80	86.66	92.87
	Girls	96.90	83.27	85.96
	Total	94.43	85.07	89.45
Middle (VI–VIII)	Boys	65.73	74.38	71.00
	Girls	49.49	65.63	74.44
	Total	58.17	70.26	73.03
High/Higher or Senior Secondary (IX–XII)	Boys	27.56	47.90	–
	Girls	18.91	39.06	–
	Total	23.49	43.76	–

Source: Calculated from the data in Table 2.8 and Census Population figures generated for the study conducted by Gill, Singh and Brar, 2005 (Table 3.9).

corresponding enrolment rate for girls has also increased from 63.69 per cent in 1971 to 96.90 per cent in 1981. However, this rate decreased to 86.66 per cent for boys and to 83.27 per cent for girls in 1991. During the period 1991–2000, these rates rose further to 92.87 per cent and 85.96 per cent for boys and girls respectively. Interestingly, gross enrolment rates in 2000 are much lower than those of in 1981. *Two*, despite the Constitutional responsibility and enactment of Compulsory Primary Education Act of 1960 in Punjab, the state has yet to achieve 100 per cent enrolment ratio for the primary age-group compared to states like Kerala and Tamil Nadu which have achieved it much earlier. *Three*, enrolment rate for girls has shown much increase as compared to boys at all levels of education. *Four*, at the high/ senior secondary levels of education, there are many differences shown in gross enrolment rates among the boys and the girls during all these years.

2.1.5 Distribution of Students

The population of students is a strong indication of the educational progress in any country. The size of the education sector is determined by the number of students directly enrolled, staff of all types, and extent of resources involved. In Triennium Ending (TE) 1980–81, out of the total student population in the state, the share of various categories of education was as follows (Table 2.11): elementary education (87.52 per cent); secondary education (9.02 per cent); university and higher education (2.80 per cent); and technical education (0.66 per cent). Within the total student population, there has been a change in the share of various sub-sectors of education. For example, the share of elementary education declined by 13.17 percentage points between TE (1980–81) and TE (2001–02). The share of secondary education went up by 11.20 percentage points during the corresponding years. However, the negligible proportion of students enrolled in technical education indicates a structural weakness in the dynamics of educational sectors which has actually been the result of faulty educational, manpower and developmental planning. This process weakens the supply of technical manpower in the system and also disturbs the associated labour market. Moreover, the leakages in the educational buildup process results in the narrowing down of the education sector at the tertiary and technical level.

Table 2.11: Distribution of Students among Various Categories of Education

Year	Ele. Edu.	Sec. Edu.	U.H.Edu.	Tech.Edu.	Edu. Overall
	1–8	9–12			
1978–81	87.52	9.02	2.80	0.66	100.00
1981–84	85.96	10.17	3.03	0.84	100.00
1984–87	85.17	10.64	3.37	0.82	100.00
1987–90	83.68	13.27	2.28	0.77	100.00
1990–93	79.93	16.76	2.60	0.72	100.00
1993–96	79.07	16.38	3.78	0.77	100.00
1996–99	77.08	18.00	4.06	0.86	100.00
1999–02	74.35	20.22	4.36	1.07	100.00

Source: Statistical Abstract of Punjab, ESO, Chandigarh (various issues).

The drastic change in the education sector in the state occurred when the share of student population was viewed within the general population (Table 2.12). The share of student population in general population declined from 19.86 per cent in TE (1980–81) to 16.89 per cent in TE (2001–02). During the corresponding years, the proportion of elementary education-level students declined from 17.38 per cent to 12.56 per cent, i.e. 4.82 percentage points. But, in case of rest of the three sub sectors the respective proportions improved. This situation needs correction as at a higher stage of development the student base of economy must be strengthened to give further impetus to the tempo of growth.

2.1.6 Disturbing Educational Outcomes

Overall, with improper handling of the education sector, the educational outcomes turned out to be highly disturbing such as high dropout rates, poor pass percentages, and presence of overage children (Table 2.13). Moreover, in the reform period, these outcomes deteriorated further, like the

Table 2.12: Share of Student Population in General Population of the Punjab

Year	Ele. Edu.	Sec. Edu.	U.H.Edu.	Tech.Edu.	Edu Overall
	1–8	9–12			
1978–81	17.38	1.79	0.56	0.13	19.86
1981–84	15.60	1.85	0.55	0.15	18.14
1984–87	15.07	1.88	0.60	0.15	17.70
1987–90	14.80	2.35	0.40	0.14	17.69
1990–93	14.65	3.07	0.48	0.13	18.32
1993–96	13.74	2.84	0.66	0.13	17.37
1996–99	13.37	3.12	0.70	0.15	17.34
1999–02	12.56	3.42	0.74	0.18	16.89

Source: 1. *Analysis of Budgeted Expenditure on Education*, MHRD, New Delhi (various issues).
2. *Statistical Abstract of Punjab*, ESO, Chandigarh (various issues).

Table 2.13: Dropout Rates and Examination Results by Education Level in State

Year	Drop-Out Rates (Percentage)			Pass Percentage in Matriculation		Share of Overage Children (2004–05)
	I–V	I–VIII	I–X	Regular Appeared Students	Private Appeared Students	
1993	22.00	39.22	48.53	–	–	Primary (12.00 per cent)
1998	21.78	27.91	42.03	65.96	41.73	
2001–02	20.33	36.99	38.62	49.18	33.53	Upper-Primary (18.19 per cent)
2002–03	25.29	32.75	48.10	–	–	

Note: Dropout rates are calculated by the Economic and Statistical Organisation, Punjab on the basis of formula suggested by CSO, Government of India in its publication, namely, *Selected Socio-Economic Statistics*, India, 1998.

Source: 1. *Economic Survey of Punjab* 1999–2000 and 2005–2006 (p.17), ESO, Chandigarh.
2. Office of Chairman, *Punjab School Education Board*, SAS Nagar, Mohali.

percentage of successfully passed out students declined from 65.96 per cent in 1998 to 49.18 per cent in 2001–03 in case of regularly appeared students in matriculation examinations. Similarly, dropout rates reached 48.10 per cent in 2002–03 from the first to tenth standard. Furthermore, for the upper-primary level, the percentage share of overage children was 18.19 in 2004–2005. The under-performance of education sector of the state is clearly reflected in the education base of the workforce of Punjab. During 1999–2000, the education level of workforce (Table 2.14) was as follows: illiterate (33.50 per cent); primary (22.10 per cent); middle (13 per cent); secondary and above (31.50 per cent) [Chadha, 2004].

There are also indications that the educational attainments of poor households fell during 1992–93 and 1998–99 across all the grades, from one to nine. For example,

Table 2.14: Distribution of Workforce as Per Principal Status in Punjab by Education Level (Based on NSSO Data)

Education Level	1999–2000			
	Primary	Secondary	Tertiary	All
Illiterate	48.3	28.2	18.3	33.5
Primary	20.8	28.9	19.4	22.1
Middle	11.2	15.7	13.6	13.0
Secondary and above	19.7	27.2	48.7	31.5
All	100	100	100	100

Source: Chadha (2004).

as many as 75 per cent of children from the top quintile households completed the 9th grade in 1998–99 compared to only 9 per cent of children from the bottom quintile households reaching the same level of grade (World Bank, 2004). Thus, the squeeze in the flow of public resources in Punjab has crippled the dynamism of the education sector, and it has got trapped in lower level of efficiency in terms of general output and quality of produce (future workforce). Hence, the whole policy package, instead of bringing about mass of quality education in the state, has resulted in the education exclusion of weaker sections of society.

2.1.7 Exclusion in Higher Education

Another serious problem of the education sector of the state is the growing exclusion of rural students from university-based education. This has emerged from the recent survey report prepared by the Punjabi University, Patiala (Tables 2.15 and 2.16). The report shows that during the academic session 2005–06, the proportion of rural students in the Universities of Punjab state and their Regional Centres was just 4.07 per cent (911 rural students out of 22,360 total students). The share of rural boys and rural girls in universities' was 4.96 per cent and 3.06 per cent, respectively.

Table 2.15: Number of Students in Universities of Punjab* (2005–06): University Campus and Regional Centre

	Total Enrolment		
	Boys	Girls	Overall
(a) Campus	9,381 (50.44)	9,217 (49.56)	18,598 (100)
(b) Regional Centres	2,560 (68.05)	1,202 (31.95)	3,762 (100)
Total (a+b)	11,941 (53.40)	10,419 (46.60)	22,360 (100)

Note: * Universities of Punjab here means four universities, viz. Punjabi University, Patiala, Panjab University, Chandigarh, Punjab Agricultural University, Ludhiana and Guru Nanak Dev University, Amritsar.
Source: *Primary Survey.*

Table 2.16: Number of Rural Students in Universities of Punjab* (2005–06): University Campus and Regional Centre

	Rural Students			Rural Students as Percentage of Total Students		
	Number					
	Boys	Girls	Overall	Boys	Girls	Overall
(a) Campus	451 (64.80)	245 (25.20)	696 (100.00)	4.81	2.66	3.74
(b) Regional Centres	141 (65.58)	74 (34.42)	215 (100.00)	5.51	6.16	5.72
Total (a+b)	592 (64.98)	319 (35.02)	911 (100.00)	4.96	3.06	4.07

Note: 1. *Universities of Punjab here means four universities, viz. Punjabi University, Patiala, Panjab University, Chandigarh, Punjab Agricultural University, Ludhiana and Guru Nanak Dev University, Amritsar.
2. Figures in parentheses are percentages.
Source: Primary Survey.

The proportion of rural students in the universities of Punjab thus is far below that of the proportion of rural population in the state (66.05 per cent, 2001). Further, the proportion of the girl students from the rural areas is rather more dismal. Amongst the total students enrolled in the universities of Punjab, the share of girl students is 46.60 per cent, whereas the share of rural girls among the total rural students is 35.20 per cent. Thus, as compared to their urban counterparts, the share of rural girls in the universities of Punjab is much lower.

2.2 Public Expenditure on Education

Punjab state's relatively higher per-capita income level is not in tune with its relatively moderate education and health indicators (Brar, 2002; Planning Commission, 2003). This situation has been the result of continuous neglect of the education sector by the state in terms of allocation of resources (Table 2.17). The perusal of data shows that the share of education sector as such in the state budgetary expenditure declined considerably over the study period of twenty-four years, i.e. 1978–79 to 2001–02. In terms of average of triennium of financial years, it declined from 23.66 per cent in 1978–81 to 16.82 per cent in 1999–02. However, its share remained in the range of 21.02 per cent to 23.66 per cent from 1978–79 to 1989–90. Afterwards it declined at a faster rate and attained its lowest level of 14.59 per cent during 1993–96. The inter-sub period comparisons established that on an average basis, the education sector got resources worth 22.08 per cent of the state budget during the first sub-period (1978–79 to 1989–90), but its share declined to 16.51 per cent during the second sub-period (1990–91 to 2001–02). Within the education sector, the share of different sub sectors declined considerably, but in case of technical education it improved marginally. It reflects the strong change in the priority of the state in terms of public spending. It is worth noting that the draft education policy of the state prepared in 2002 makes no mention of the availability of resources (GoP, 2002).

2.2.1 Education Budget, State Income and General Budget

The withdrawal of the state from the education sector becomes further clear when education budget has been

Table 2.17: Level and Percentage Share of Public Expenditure on Education and its Different Categories in Punjab State's Overall Budgetary Expenditure (Revenue Account) (Plan plus Non-Plan) (Figures in Rs. Crore)

(Triennium Average)	Elementary Education	Secondary Education	Technical Education	University Higher Education	Others	Education (Overall)
1978–81	39.69 (8.64)	50.70 (11.04)	1.28 (0.28)	12.59 (2.74)	4.39 (0.96)	108.65 (23.66)
1981–84	55.70 (7.87)	80.42 (11.36)	2.14 (0.30)	20.30 (2.87)	6.14 (0.87)	164.71 (23.27)
1984–87	77.80 (7.06)	110.96 (10.07)	3.25 (0.30)	31.71 (2.88)	7.96 (0.72)	231.68 (21.02)
1987–90	131.90 (7.17)	201.35 (10.94)	4.39 (0.24)	58.75 (3.19)	5.91 (0.32)	402.30 (21.86)
1990–93	180.31 (5.39)	288.71 (8.63)	14.26 (0.43)	79.36 (2.37)	7.33 (0.22)	569.98 (17.05)
1993–96	252.95 (4.84)	375.27 (7.18)	15.38 (0.29)	105.61 (2.02)	13.11 (0.25)	762.33 (14.59)
1996–99	394.30 (5.11)	376.79 (9.55)	36.22 (0.47)	141.06 (1.83)	12.95 (0.17)	1321.32 (17.13)
1999–02	603.43 (5.12)	1104.91 (9.37)	52.07 (0.44)	207.14 (1.76)	15.63 (0.13)	1983.18 (16.82)
Average Annual: Ist Sub period (1978–79 to 1989–90)	76.27 (7.42)	110.86 (10.79)	2.76 (0.27)	30.84 (3.00)	6.10 (0.59)	226.84 (22.08)
Average Annual: IInd Sub period (1990–91 to 2001–02)	357.74 (5.10)	626.42 (8.92)	29.48 (0.42)	133.29 (1.90)	12.26 (0.17)	1159.20 (16.51)

Note: 1. Figures presented are triennium averages of concerned financial years.
2. Figures in parentheses refer to the percentage share in state budget.

Source: *Analysis of Budgeted Expenditure on Education*, MHRD, New Delhi (various issues).

analyzed according to the various developmental Plans (Table 2.18). The table presents the data specific to four Plans each of five years' duration and one of two years' duration. The share of education in state budget declined consistently. Its average share was 23.31 per cent during the Sixth Plan (1980–85), which went down to 14.41 per cent during the Ninth Plan (1992–97). Similarly, the proportion of education budget into state income too declined in the successive plans ending in March 1997. However, it improved to 17.24 per cent during 1997–02, mainly on account of grade revision specific to this period. This is also clear from the share of non-plan component (89 per cent) in the overall educational budget, as well as that of revenue account (99.57 per cent) during 1997–02. Furthermore, resource experience of education sector becomes clearer when it is examined on the basis of per-student allocation in real terms (Table 2.19). The education sector (overall) on per-student real basis experienced a growth rate of 5.99 per cent per annum during the first sub-period (i.e. 1978–79 to 1989–90), which declined to 5.55 per cent during the second sub-period (i.e. 1990–91 to 2001–02). Technical education, and university and higher education too experienced a decline on per-student real basis while the elementary and secondary education experienced a rise on per-student basis. This happened because of less growth of students during the reform period in these cases. However, resources to the education sector in real terms on per-student basis increased by 3.89 per cent per annum during 1978–79 to 2001–02. The growing dominance of spending on activities other than education during the reform period has thus been quite pronounced.

2.2.2 Inter-Sectoral Education Expenditure

Another special feature of the education budget of the state is that more than half of it was consumed by the secondary

Table 2.18: Certain Features of Education Budget of State According to Various Five-Year and Annual Plan Periods

Plan Period	Percentage Share in State Budget	Percentage Share in State Income	Division of Education Budget into		Share in Education Budget	
			R.A.	C.A.	Plan	Non-Plan
1980–85 (6th Plan)	23.31	2.88	99.05	0.95	6.06	93.94
1985–90 (7th Plan)	21.44	3.02	98.63	1.37	5.16	94.84
1990–92 (Annual Plan)	15.55	2.84	100.00	0.00	3.97	96.03
1992–97 (8th Plan)	14.41	2.42	98.59	1.41	11.13	88.87
1997–02 (9th Plan)	17.24	3.31	99.57	0.43	12.30	87.70

Note: R.A. stands for Revenue Account and C.A. for Current Account.
Source: *Analysis of Budgeted Expenditure on Education*, MHRD, New Delhi (various issues).

Table 2.19: Per-Student Real Growth of Educational Expenditure in the State

Year	Elementary Education	Secondary Education	Technical Education	U.H. Education	Education (Overall)
1978–79 to 1989–90	5.42	2.44	4.08	10.06	5.99
1990–91 to 2001–02	5.62	4.69	2.96	–3.81	5.55
1978–79 to 2001–02	3.90	0.63	7.13	1.17	3.89

Note: Real growth has been worked out by using the NSDP-deflator with 1993–94 = 100 as base.
Source: 1. Analysis *of Budgeted Expenditure on Education*, MHRD, New Delhi (various issues).
2. *Statistical Abstract of Punjab*, Chandigarh (various issues).

education alone (Table 2.20). The share of this sector gradually went up from 46.67 per cent to 55.71 per cent, respectively from 1978–81 to 1999–02. The corresponding shares of elementary education, university and higher

Table 2.20: Percentage Distribution of Educational Expenditure into Various Categories of Education (Revenue Account Only)

Year	Elementary Education	Secondary Education	Technical Education	U.H.Edu.	Others	Education (Overall)
1978–81	36.53	46.67	1.17	11.59	4.04	100
1981–84	33.82	48.83	1.30	12.32	3.73	100
1984–87	33.58	47.90	1.40	13.69	3.43	100
1987–90	32.79	50.50	1.09	14.60	1.47	100
1990–93	31.63	50.65	2.50	13.92	1.29	100
1993–96	33.18	49.23	2.02	13.85	1.72	100
1996–99	29.84	55.76	2.74	10.68	0.98	100
1999–02	30.43	55.71	2.63	10.44	0.79	100

Source: *Analysis of Budgeted Expenditure on Education*, MHRD, New Delhi, (various issues).

education and the category called 'others' declined. However, there has been an improvement in the share of technical education. The relative change in the share of various sub sectors has disturbed the resource equilibrium position of the sub sectors.

2.2.3 Plan and Non-Plan Expenditure

Apart from the overall size of the education budget, its very composition in terms of Plan and non-Plan break-up determines the growth of the educational system. Under the Plan component, the capital formation takes place and possibility of new infrastructure generation arises, while the non-Plan expenditure has been used for the running and maintenance of the existing activities. The share of Plan component was very low in case of all categories as well as overall level of education (Tables 2.21 and 2.22). During the study period, i.e. T.E. (1980–81) to T.E (2001–02), the share of Plan component remained very low. It declined to its lowest level (3.85 per cent) in TE (1986–87), and rose to 12.32 per cent during TE (2001–02) in case of overall education budget. The non-Plan expenditure

Table 2.21: Plan and Non-plan Break-up of Public Expenditure on Various Categories of Education (Revenue Account) (Rs. Crore)

Year	Elementary Education		Secondary Education		Education Overall	
	PI	N.PI	PI	N.PI	PI	N.PI
1978–81	1.05 (2.65)	38.64 (97.35)	4.66 (9.19)	46.04 (90.81)	7.91 (7.28)	100.74 (92.72)
1981–84	0.11 (0.19)	55.60 (99.81)	7.75 (9.64)	72.67 (90.36)	10.11 (6.14)	154.60 (93.86)
1984–87	0.47 (0.60)	77.33 (99.40)	5.60 (5.05)	105.36 (94.95)	8.92 (3.85)	222.76 (96.15)
1987–90	3.34 (2.53)	128.56 (97.47)	15.65 (7.77)	185.71 (92.23)	25.10 (6.24)	377.20 (93.76)
1990–93	4.81 (2.67)	175.50 (97.33)	23.14 (8.02)	265.57 (91.98)	36.76 (6.45)	533.22 (93.55)
1993–96	6.80 (2.69)	246.14 (97.31)	51.71 (13.78)	323.56 (86.22)	75.70 (9.93)	686.62 (90.07)
1996–99	1.58 (0.40)	392.71 (99.60)	131.90 (17.90)	604.89 (82.10)	157.63 (11.93)	1163.69 (88.07)
1999–2002	1.84 (0.30)	601.59 (99.70)	208.77 (18.89)	896.14 (81.11)	244.33 (12.32)	1738.85 (87.68)

Note: 1. Figures in parenthesis are percentages of the respective category.
2. The table does not show the break-up of Plan and non-Plan expenditure in the case of 'Others' and hence the total expenditure on education shown here is not equal to the expenditure of the four categories shown.

Source: *Analysis of Budgeted Expenditure on Education*, MHRD, New Delhi (various issues).

constituted 87.68 per cent of the education budget during TE (2001–02). The Plan-expenditure during the decade of the1990s, on an average, was higher than that of the1980s. The Plan component was found to be relatively on a much lower side in proportionate terms than that of non-Plan components in case of elementary education than the rest. It was just 0.30 per cent in TE (2001–02). So, in this category of education about 99 per cent of the budget has been used under the non-Plan mode of expenditure. In the case of secondary education, the position in the later years of the study improved and the share of Plan expenditure reached to 14 per cent in TE (1995–96), and to about 19 per cent in

Table 2.22: Plan and Non-plan Break-up of Public Expenditure on Various Categories of Education (Revenue Account) (Rs. Crore)

Year	Technical Education		U.H. Ed		Education Overall	
	PI	N.PI	PI	N.PI	PI	N.PI
1978–81	0.15 (12.01)	1.12 (87.99)	0.92 (7.28)	11.67 (92.72)	7.91 (7.28)	100.74 (92.72)
1981–84	0.23 (10.59)	1.91 (89.41)	0.52 (2.56)	19.78 (97.44)	10.11 (6.14)	154.60 (93.86)
1984–87	0.81 (25.00)	2.44 (75.00)	0.81 (2.57)	30.89 (97.43)	8.92 (3.85)	222.76 (96.15)
1987–90	1.30 (29.71)	3.08 (70.29)	4.15 (7.06)	54.60 (92.94)	25.10 (6.24)	377.20 (93.76)
1990–93	6.95 (48.74)	7.31 (51.26)	1.12 (1.42)	78.24 (98.58)	36.76 (6.45)	533.22 (93.55)
1993–96	7.78 (50.60)	7.60 (49.40)	7.42 (7.03)	98.19 (92.97)	75.70 (9.93)	686.62 (90.07)
1996–99	20.70 (57.15)	15.52 (42.85)	2.60 (1.84)	138.46 (98.16)	157.63 (11.93)	1163.69 (88.07)
1999–02	31.57 (60.63)	20.50 (39.37)	0.93 (0.45)	206.21 (99.55)	244.33 (12.32)	1738.85 (87.68)

Note: 1. Figures in parenthesis are percentages of the respective category.
2. The table does not show the break-up of Plan and non-Plan expenditure in the case of 'Others' and hence the total expenditure on education shown here is not equal to the expenditure of the four categories shown.

Source: *Analysis of Budgeted Expenditure on Education*, MHRD, New Delhi (various issues).

TE (2001–02). The Plan component was found to be quite on the higher side in case of the technical education. During the decade of the1990s, its average share was more than 50 per cent, and during TE (2001–02) it was about 61 per cent. However, in case of university and higher education, the Plan component turned out to be very low, i.e. just 0.45 per cent in TE (2001–02).

2.2.4 Per -Student and Per-Capita Expenditure

The spending priorities could be very aptly captured by examining the expenditure on per-capita and per-student basis. The per-student expenditure at current prices witnessed a rise consistently (Table 2.23). It rose from Rs. 346.99 during TE (1980–81), to Rs. 1,173.03 during TE (1989–90), and ultimately to Rs. 4,755.19 during TE (2001–02). Similarly, it increased during all of the mentioned trienniums in case of elementary and secondary education. But, it also witnessed in its level a dip than from the respective preceding years in case of technical and university and higher education, during TE (1995–96). Further, the per-student expenditure was found to be lowest in case of elementary education than those of the other categories. The per-student expenditure during TE (2001–02) was 13.71 times more than that of TE (1980–81), in the case of overall education.

The education expenditure on per-capita basis (Table 2.24) increased overall from Rs. 68.90 during TE (1980–81) to Rs. 803.16 during TE (2001–02). It was highest in case of secondary education and lowest in case of technical education, respectively being Rs. 447.47 and Rs. 21.09 during TE (2001–02). The interesting feature, which emerges from comparison, is that during TE (2001–02), the per-capita income of the state was Rs. 24184.33. So, per capita

Table 2.23: Per-Student Expenditure on Various Categories of Education (Rupee) (Current Prices)

Year	Ele. Edu.	Sec. Edu.	Tec. Edu.	U.H. Edu.	Edu. Overall
1978–81	144.82	1795.87	616.37	1436.79	346.99
1981–84	209.44	2555.83	821.49	2165.23	532.33
1984–87	281.58	3215.35	1218.51	2900.15	714.15
1987–90	459.58	4423.77	1666.39	7524.37	1173.03
1990–93	603.95	4612.72	5339.02	8177.23	1525.98
1993–96	841.28	6026.40	5232.72	7351.58	2004.83
1996–99	1259.99	10084.10	10327.82	8557.44	3254.56
1999–2002	1946.01	13099.56	11720.57	11393.28	4755.19

Source: 1. *Analysis of Budgeted Expenditure on Education*, MHRD, New Delhi (various issues).
2. *Statistical Abstract of Punjab*, ESO, Chandigarh (various issues)

Table 2.24: Per-Capita Public Expenditure on Various Categories of Education

Year	Ele. Edu.	Sec. Edu.	Tec. Edu.	U.H. Edu.	Edu. Overall
1978–81	25.17	32.15	0.81	7.98	68.90
1981–84	32.66	47.16	1.25	11.90	96.59
1984–87	42.44	60.53	1.77	17.29	126.37
1987–90	68.04	103.86	2.26	30.30	207.52
1990–93	88.46	141.64	7.00	38.94	279.63
1993–96	115.56	171.44	7.03	48.25	348.27
1996–99	168.43	314.73	15.47	60.25	564.41
1999–2002	244.38	447.47	21.09	83.89	803.16

Source: 1. *Analysis of Budgeted Expenditure on Education*, MHRD, New Delhi (various issues).
2. *Statistical Abstract of Punjab*, ESO, Chandigarh (various issues).

education spending constituted 3.32 per cent of per capita state income.

Thus, the public spending on education in the state was not in tune with its educational requirements, particularly in the context of weak educational outcomes and emerging challenges of human capital formation. The inadequacy of educational spending has also been reflected in the context of national norms and expert consensus pertaining to the desired proportion of state income. There have been significant distortions in the budget of the education sector with less availability of funds for capital and Plan account. The post-reform period witnessed a fall in the share of education budget to state budget to a significant extent. The limited increase in education budget in real terms has in effect converted and reduced the education budget into a salary budget. Out of this inadequate budget, more than half goes to secondary education, and the rest to other sectors of education. The system of education witnessed a shift towards private players at all stages and types of education. This has created its own sort of momentum and generated disequilibrium in the process of governance and policy interventions. With this style of education delivery system the students, parents and staff in the large number of unregulated private sector have been pushed to margin and placed at the receiving end. The unchecked growth, tuition fees and funds, and non-functionality of government schools have generated educational exclusion for the rural, weaker sections, and first-generation learners. Therefore, educational governance has to be crafted on sound parameters to enhance the delivery mechanism to ensure educational effectiveness and inclusion.

3

Health Services in Punjab

The role of health services in the socio-economic development of a country is well documented in economic literature, mainly on two counts. First, these services help to keep people healthy, both physically and mentally, by preventing occurrence of diseases, and providing treatment in the case of illnesses/diseases (Mushkin, 1962; World Bank, 1993 and Misra, R. et al., 2003). Second, these services enhance the longevity of people's life, especially of the poor, by (i) increasing their labour supply lost due to occurrence of diseases/illnesses (Grossman and Benham, 1974), and (ii) enhancing the economic opportunities for greater earnings or higher productivity (Luft, 1975; Strauss and Duncan, 1995). Mainstream growth economists and institutions, in unison, emphasize the public provision of health services not only to provide low cost and quality treatment in case people suffer from diseases/illnesses, but also to promote health status by preventing occurrence of diseases among people.

Recognizing the vital importance of improved health to lead a better quality of life, the World Health Organisation (WHO) states that access to healthcare is everybody's right (WHO, 1996). And, there is a widespread consensus among all the world countries that the allocation of more public funds is the best way to develop an effective and efficient public health system that promotes and helps in the maintenance of human health. The main reasons that are often cited in favour of public health interventions are the 'market failure' in the purchase and provision of health services; 'achieving equity' in heath outcomes; and 'imperfect information' on the part of people about the nature of health problems and corresponding treatment processes (Grosh and Glewwe, 2000). Moreover, public expenditure on the health sector also produces a number of externalities in the form of improving child survival rate, promoting women's health, and reducing population growth in the country (World Bank, 1993).

The present chapter analyzes the impacts of globalization on health and the health delivery system in one of the progressive states of India, i.e. Punjab. In Punjab, the health services along with the education continue to be one of the pillars of developing human resources and economic reconstruction of the state economy (Gill and Ghuman, 2000). During the 1970s and the mid-1980s, more public funds were pumped to develop health services in the state sector (Singh, 2005). The state, being one of the highly developed states of India, has the capacity to invest more and its people are expected to have better health levels compared to other major states of India. However, the Southern states, like Kerala and Tamil Nadu despite their low per-capita incomes, have been able to achieve much improved education and health-related indicators than that of Punjab (Brar, 2002). Since the mid-1980s due to the political turmoil, severe resource crunch and non-responsive administration in the state on one hand, and the adoption of the new economic policy (NEP) of 1991 at the national level that emphasizes the integration of nation's economy into world economy through the forces of liberalization, privatization and globalization (LPG), on the other, public investment in social sectors, especially the public health sector in Punjab, has gradually been withdrawn. This has led to a faster deterioration in the public health infrastructure and services, particularly in rural Punjab (Singh, 2005).

This chapter has been divided into five parts. Part I analyzes, in brief, the theoretical implications of globalization on the health sector of the state. Part II, in the light of these implications, examines the growth and pattern of public expenditure on health services in Punjab. Part III deals with the main characteristics of health care infrastructure developed so far in the state. The non-functional and dismal performance of rural health services has been presented in Part IV. Finally, a summary of main conclusions and emerging issues are set forth in Part V.

I

3.1 Globalization and the Health Sector: Theoretical Underpinnings

Globalization, in its true essence, is defined as the growing process of economic interdependence of nation-states through the increasing volume and variety of cross-border transactions of goods and services, free movement of capital, people, ideas and knowledge, and more important, the widespread diffusion of new technology at an astonishing speed. From this, it appears that globalization has economic, political, technological, and cultural dimensions that are interwoven with one another and affect the main activities of nation-states. But, defining globalization as mere 'openness of economy' does not convey and capture the multiple, often contradictory, contours of real forces/ mechanisms that are at play among the nation-states.

The process of integrating a nation's economy with world economy affects the people's health and health delivery system both positively/negatively and directly/ indirectly. Its impacts may be observed in the range of highly positive health outcomes (better incomes, better living conditions, access to better health technology/medicine to prevent/control diseases, high life expectancy, etc.) to highly deleterious effects on health (high treatment costs, elite-oriented policies, high incidence of man-made diseases, irrational use of drugs/technology, etc.). Globalization directly influences a nation's health mainly through: (i) the enhanced movement of pharmaceutical products, health personnel and patients across the national boundaries; (ii) the elite-oriented health consumerism and medical tourism via the Internet and other means; and (iii) the establishment of big corporate hospitals having Five Star facilities. Besides, more mobility of people increases the chances of spreading of diseases across borders. Further, globalization, if accompanied by low public funds to the health sector, plays havoc with the health of the poor in developing countries (Baum, 2001).

On the other side, in an indirect way, globalization affects the people's health in most of developing countries through the heightened industrial activities, depletion of natural resources, indiscriminate use of insecticides/pesticides and increasing environmental pollution (air and water pollution) due to unsafe disposal of untreated industrial waste. Moreover, high consumption of tobacco/alcoholic products, rising consumption of packed/frozen foods and aerated beverages also affect the people's health negatively. The emergence of high-risk diseases like diabetes, cancer, heart disease, and other life-style diseases (TB, HIV/AIDS, etc.) can be linked to the global economic policies. Moreover, the resource poor people, falling prey to high-risk chronic and lifestyle diseases means less employment, and subsequently the poverty and malnourishment of women/children in the family, which is also attributed to globalization by some authors (Cornia, 2001; Chatterjee, 2007).

In India, during the early 1990s, with the formal acceptance of the structural adjustment programme (SAP), integration of Indian economy with global economy became a reality. In fact, the imposition of SAP has considerably reduced state investment in the social sectors, including the health sector in India. In public health fields, the role of the state has increasingly been marginalized. Further, health sector reforms piloted by the World Bank in India are actively promoting private-sector initiatives, giving more emphasis to non-governmental bodies, contracting out, and suggesting other forms of organization (Public-Private Partnership) in health management. In a nutshell, the main aspects of IMF-World Bank inspired health reforms in India are: cuts in health sector investments, opening up of healthcare to the private sector, levying of users' charges, contracting out some services of public hospitals and stressing of purely techno-centric public health interventions (Qadeer, 2000).

Due to the cutbacks in health sector funds, the primary healthcare services suffered a major setback. For want of more funds, infectious diseases control programmes were disrupted and family welfare programme began to focus on the reproductive health of married women only. By handing over healthcare to private sector players, without any regulatory mechanism to ensure the quality and standards of treatment, the state is withdrawing itself from the Constitutional obligations and seriously affecting the equal access of health services to the marginalized section of society (Baru, 1998).

II

3.2 Rationale for Public Spending

Public expenditure on health is a powerful instrument of

fiscal policy, inter alia, to improve the socio-economic welfare of people. A perusal of recently produced economic literature related to development economics mirrors that the developing countries are investing more public funds in the social sector programmes, namely health, fertility control and education (Walle and Nead, 1995). An earlier study also states that shifts in the pattern of public expenditure towards social sectors represent one of the most effective techniques with the government to improve the living conditions of the poor and, also, the re-distribution of public services (Wulf, 1975). The analysis of relative shifts in development expenditure incurred on different social and economic services seems to be rather rewarding because the expenditures on these services have affected the people's life differently than for which such expenditures are intended to be made. And, in India, the global forces have affected the allocation of public funds not only to the health sector as a whole, but also within the health sector (Qadeer, 2000). This has distorted the priority status of many health care programmes, mainly due to the cuts in public health sector's investment, donor-driven priorities and emphasis on privatization of health care. Interestingly, Punjab's health sector plan is largely dependent upon the Union Government both for the finances and policy matters (Singh, 2005).

3.2.1 Public Expenditure on Health Services

An assessment of sectoral allocation of public expenditure in Punjab is, therefore, necessary because the state health sector under the new economic policy of LPG has to compete with other urgent development and non-development services. In Punjab, the analysis of public expenditure on health including family welfare (FW) services on revenue account (Table 3.1) reveals that, although the total expenditure on these services in real terms has spiralled from Rs. 138.81 crore during the triennium period of

Table 3.1: Distribution of Public Expenditure from Revenue Account by Major Heads in Punjab

(Figures in Rs. Crore at 1993–94 prices)

Triennium Period	Total Expenditure	Non-Development Expenditure	Development Expenditure	Social Services Only	Health & Family Welfare	Health & Family Welfare as Percentage of			Per-Capita Expenditure Rs.
						Social Services	Development Expenditure	NSDP	
1978–79 to 1980–81	1520.24 (100.00	410.71 (26.66)	1109.54 (73.34)	625.73 (41.00)	139.81 (9.30)	22.34	12.68	1.08	87
1981–82 to 1983–84	1889.60 (100.00)	571.45 (30.67)	1318.14 (69.33)	741.97 (39.00)	172.42 (8.98)	23.24	12.95	1.29	101
1984–85 to 1986–87	2383.50 (100.00)	837.89 (34.51)	1545.62 (65.49)	932.16 (39.48)	211.71 (9.18)	22.71	14.01	0.99	117
1987–88 to 1989–90	2994.60 (100.00)	955.39 (30.69)	2039.17 (69.31)	1330.45 (45.01)	215.49 (6.97)	16.20	10.05	0.82	112
1990–91 to 1992–93	4025.37 (100.00)	1365.99 (31.28)	2689.78 (69.67)	1153.73 (28.25)	223.34 (5.46)	19.36	7.83	0.75	110
1993–94 to 1995–96	4686.01 (100.00)	2676.80 (59.06)	2009.18 (40.94)	1161.97 (24.06)	214.95 (4.35)	18.50	10.62	0.89	100
1996–97 to 1998–99	5537.74 (100.00)	2697.89 (50.14)	2839.84 (49.86)	1476.69 (27.65)	292.82 (5.48)	19.83	10.98	0.91	124
1999–2000 to 2001–03	7044.19 (100.00)	4108.59 (58.98)	2935.60 (41.02)	1780.51 (24.97)	371.05 (5.23)	19.84	11.76	0.87	154
2002–03 to 2004–05	9152.56 (100.00)	5395.67 (60.24)	3756.89 (39.76)	1992.08 (21.67)	371.73 (4.02)	18.66	10.12	0.81	147

Note: Figures in parentheses are percentage shares.

Source: *Statistical Abstract of Punjab*, (various issues), Economic Advisor to Government of Punjab.

1978–79 to 1980–81 to Rs. 371.73 crore during the triennium period of 2002–03 to 2004–05, yet, in relative terms, the share of the health sector out of the total budgetary expenditure, development expenditure and state income has shown a decreasing trend. For instance, the share of health sector remained around 9 per cent between the triennium period of 1978–79 to 1980–81 and the triennium period of 1984–85 to 1986–87. Thereafter, it decreased to 6.97 per cent during the triennium period of 1987–88 to 1989–90, 5.46 per cent during the triennium period of 1990–91 to 1992–93, 4.35 per cent during the triennium period of 1993–94 to 1995–96; again it slightly rose to 5.48 per cent during the triennium period of 1996–97 to 1998–99 and fell to 4.02 per cent during the triennium period of 2002–03 to 2004–05. A similar picture emerged when one viewed the share of the health sector as the proportion to total development expenditure and social services in the state. Further, as the percentage of NSDP, **the share of health services in Punjab never reached one per cent for most of years against the normative ratio of 3 per cent of the state/national income**. This shows that the public expenditure on health sector has experienced a decelerated growth over the time period, especially after the initiation of NEP of 1991 (post-reforms period) in India.

3.2.2 Intra-Sectoral Planned Health Expenditure

Theoretically, the allocation of more public funds to the health sector is of paramount importance, particularly to improve its accessibility and relevance to the poor sections of society. But, in practice, the intra-sectoral allocations (expenditure) within the health sector are also very important and useful to determine the changing health priorities of the state, if any. However, the programme-wise disaggregated data of total public health expenditure in Punjab are not available, except for the planned expenditure during different Plan periods. The study looked at the detailed breakdown of planned health expenditure to judge the priority programmes/schemes adopted during the different Plan periods (Table 3.2). The data reveal that a very high proportion of total health sector's planned expenditure incurred on a single programme, that is, the FW programme. The share of FW programme that was 34.57 per cent in the Sixth Five Year Plan (1980–85) decreased to 28.92 per cent in the Seventh Five Year Plan (1985–90) and rose to 30.84 per cent in the Eighth Five Year Plan (1992–07). Then it decreased to 21.56 per cent during the Ninth Five Year Plan (1997–2002) and the allocation rose to 33.73 per cent during the Tenth Five Year Plan (2002–07). Establishment and strengthening of new/old hospitals, PHCs, dispensaries, etc. received second priority status programme, mainly owing to the rural health component of Minimum Needs Programme. Under this head, a little more than one-fourth (25.56 per cent) of total health plan expenditure was incurred during the Sixth Five Year Plan (1980–85), more than one-half (56.33 per cent) during the Ninth Five Year Plan (1997–2002) and a little less than two-fifth (37.46 per cent) during the Tenth Five Year Plan (2002–07).

Control/eradication of communicable diseases is another major component of public health plan expenditure up to the Eighth Five Year Plan (1992–97). Plan expenditure under this head was 13.46 per cent during the Sixth Five Year Plan (1980–85) and rose to 27.03 per cent during the Seventh Five Year Plan (1985–90), but declined to 10.95 per cent during the Eighth Five Year Plan (1992–97). During the Ninth Five Year Plan (1997–2002) and Tenth Five Year Plan (2002–07), this head had just 0.83 per cent and 2.48 per cent share in the allocation of funds respectively. On the other hand, medical education, research and training consistently decreased their share in relative terms from 14.62 per cent during the Sixth Five Year Plan (1980–85) to 11.27 per cent during the Seventh Five Year Plan (1985–90), 10.87 per cent during the Eighth Five Year Plan (1992–97) and 5.84 per cent during the Ninth Five Year Plan (1997–2002). During the Tenth Five Year Plan (2002–07), there was a proposal to spend 14.03 per cent of total health plan allocations on this head. This posed very serious repercussions on the doctors' training, developing core competencies among them and deterioration in tertiary healthcare provided by the hospitals attached with government-owned medical colleges of the state. Moreover, it is quite interesting that the indigenous systems of medicine (Ayurvedic) and homeopathy are being continuously neglected, at least, in terms of allocation of plan funds in Punjab. Also, the Employees' State Insurance Scheme did not find any priority status (Table 3.2).

The Constitutional division of powers between the centre and the states in India clearly shows that the state governments have exclusive jurisdictional powers to establish and monitor the provision for the 'public health and sanitation', 'hospitals and dispensaries' and 'burials and cremations' in their respective areas. The role of central government is limited largely to the regulation of medical standards, formulation of health policy, regulation of international health issues, giving policy directions and allocation of more finances for strategic health programmes/ schemes (Prakash and Raj, 1972). Thus, in theory, creating provisions for healthcare is largely a state subject, but in practice the central government plays a very significant role through financing states' health sector plans.

An analysis of data (Table 3.3) reveals that the central government financed a greater part of Punjab's planned health expenditure; 47.62 per cent during the Sixth Five Year Plan (1980–85), 57.83 per cent during the Seventh Five Year Plan (1985–90), 59.57 per cent during the Eighth Five Year Plan (1992–97) and 39.99 per cent during the Tenth Five Year Plan (2002–07). The data also illustrate that all the priority

Table 3.2: Planed Expenditure on Health and Family Welfare in Punjab during different Plan Periods

(Figures in Rs. Crore at 1993–94 prices)

Major Head	Annual Plan (1979–80)	Sixth Five Year Plan (1980–85)	Seventh Five Year Plan (1985–90)	Annual Plan (1990–92)	Eighth Five Year Plan (1992–97)	Ninth Five Year Plan (1997–02)	Tenth Five Year Plan (2002–07)
(i) Medical Education, Research & Training	5.50 (12.32)	38.69 (14.62)	31.11 (11.27)	17.78 (11.21)	30.56 (10.87)	22.75 (5.84)	66.68 (14.03)
(ii) Establishment & Strengthening of Hospitals, CHCs/PHCs, SHCs *	8.28 (18.55)	67.66** (25.56)	52.01 (18.85)	34.13 (21.53)	76.55 (27.23)	219.28 (56.33)	178.04 (37.46)
(iii) Control/Eradication of Communicable Diseases	10.94 (24.51)	35.62 (13.46)	74.59 (27.03)	14.95 (9.43)	30.80 (10.95)	3.23 (0.83)	11.79 (2.48)
(iv) Indigenous Systems of Medicine & Homeopathy	0.62 (1.40)	6.19 (2.34)	3.24 (1.18)	1.86 (1.17)	6.74 (2.40)	3.02 (0.78)	9.05 (1.90)
(v) Other Programmes to Strengthen Delivery System	5.34 (11.96)	23.51 (8.88)	34.39 (12.46)	35.06 ** (22.11)	49.79 (17.71)	57.06 (14.66)	49.43 (10.40)
Health Proper (I to v)	30.84 (69.08)	173.17 (65.43)	196.17 (71.08)	104.05 (65.62)	194.49 (69.16)	305.35 (78.44)	314.99 (66.27)
Family Welfare	13.80 (30.92)	91.49 (34.57)	79.81 (28.92)	54.52 (34.38)	86.71 (30.84)	83.90 (21.56)	160.30 (33.73)
Total (Health and Family Welfare)	44.64 (100.00)	264.67 (100.00)	275.98 (100.00)	158.57 (100.00)	281.20 (100.00)	389.25 (100.00)	475.29 (100.00)

Note: * It includes the contribution under the Minimum Needs Programme.

** It includes USAID-Assisted Area Projects.

Figures in parentheses are percentage shares.

Source: *Plan Document*, Department of Planning, Government of Punjab (various issues).

Table 3.3: Central Government Versus State Government's Share in Total Health and Family Welfare Plan Expenditure in Punjab during Different Five Year Plans

(Rs. in Crores at 1993–94 Prices)

Plan Periods	Total Plan Expenditure on Health and Family Welfare	Central Government's Share				State Government's Share			
		Family Welfare Alone	Control of Communicable Diseases	Other Programmes	Sub-Total	Family Welfare	Control of Communicable Diseases	Others Programmes	Sub-Total
Annual Plans (1979–80)	44.64 (100.00)	13.80 (30.92)	7.50 (16.81)	3.99 (8.93)	25.29 (56.65)	0.00 (0.00)	3.44 (7.70)	15.91 (35.64)	19.35 (43.34)
Sixth Five Year Plan (1980–85)	264.67 (100.00)	85.64 (32.36)	18.57 (7.02)	21.84 (8.25)	126.05 (47.62)	5.86 (2.21)	17.05 (6.44)	115.72 (43.72)	138.62 (52.38)
Seventh Five Year Plan (1985–90)	275.98 (100.00)	79.45 (28.79)	41.45 (15.02)	38.70 (14.02)	159.59 (57.83)	0.36 (0.13)	33.14 (12.01)	82.88 (30.03)	116.38 (42.17)
Annual Plans (1990–92)	158.57 (100.00)	54.52 (34.38)	7.44 (4.69)	31.27 (19.72)	93.23 (58.79)	0.00 (0.00)	7.51 (4.74)	58.09 (36.63)	65.34 (41.21)
Eighth Five Year Plan (1992–97)	281.20 (100.00)	86.71 (30.84)	16.82 (5.98)	63.98 (22.75)	167.52 (59.57)	0.00 (0.00)	13.97 (4.97)	99.70 (35.46)	113.68 (40.43)
Ninth Five Year Plan (1997–2002)	389.25 (100.00)	93.90 (21.56)	1.79 (0.46)	5.54 (1.42)	91.23 (23.44)	0.00 (0.00)	1.45 (0.37)	296.5 (76.19)	298.02 (76.56)
Tenth Five Year Plan (2002–07)	475.29 (100.00)	160.30 (33.73)	5.40 (1.14)	24.36 (5.13)	190.00 (39.99)	0.00 (0.00)	0.39 (1.34)	278.86 (58.67)	285.23 (60.01)

Note: Figures in parentheses are percentage shares.
Source: *Plan Document*, Department of Planning, Government of Punjab (various issues).

programmes of state health plan, like the family welfare and control of communicable diseases, got more allocation of central funds, mainly due to the policy of the central government to promote these programmes. Among these priority programmes, the FW is fully central funded programme and in the case of two other programmes, liberal central grants along with matching contributions by the state are made available. The Punjab government utilized these grants to expand healthcare and family welfare infrastructure in the state.

Establishment of hospitals, PHCs, dispensaries, etc. comprises other priority programmes in Punjab's health sector plan. Again, under this head, sufficient central funds are allocated to finance these programmes. Actually, this is one of the main reasons why these programmes have emerged as priority programmes in the state's health plans. In the case of eradicating communicable diseases, the central government spent more funds, both absolutely and relatively, compared to the funds made available by the state government (Table 3.3). Further, 'other programmes' under the state category, which consist of minimum needs programme, hospitals and dispensaries, medical education, etc. deal with the creation and strengthening of infrastructure facilities in the state. These programmes are crucial health programmes for the maintenance of the health of the people. These are financed partly by the central government and partly by the state from its own resources. The state's share under this head remained around 44 per cent in the Sixth Five Year Plan (1980–85) and decreased to 30.03 per cent in the Seventh Five Year Plan (1985–90), but rose to 35.46 per cent in the Eighth Five Year Plan (1992–97) and 76.19 per cent in the Ninth Five Year Plan (1997–2002), and declined to 58.67 per cent in the Tenth Five Year Plan (2002–07). Thus, state is highly dependent on central government for finances as well as health policy matters. The main conclusion that emerged from this is that whenever there is a policy shift at the all-India level, it is automatically reflected at the states level. Indeed, this is true in the case of the health sector of Punjab.

III

3.3 Health Delivery System in Punjab

Public and private providers dominate the health delivery system of the state. In large urban towns of Punjab, hospitals attached with the medical colleges provide tertiary health care facilities. In medium/smaller towns and some larger villages, the state government runs an extensive infrastructure of district hospitals, tehsil hospitals; community health centres (CHCs) and rural hospitals (RHs). A network of CHCs/RHs, PHCs and dispensaries has been serving the rural people. Theoretically, the state health delivery system is operating at three levels: (i) at the primary level, (CHC, PHCs and dispensaries); (ii) at the secondary level, (district and tehsil hospitals); and (iii) at the tertiary level (medical college hospitals and central government hospitals). On the other hand, an overwhelming majority of private health providers dominantly provide clinic/office-based practice of general practitioners, and mostly concentrate on low-risk cases. An overwhelming majority of them are based in urban areas.

3.3.1 Stagnation in Public Health Infrastructure

In Punjab, public health facilities increased up to the mid-1980s mainly due to the increased allocation of funds to the state health sector and the pro-rural policy of the state government (Singh, 2005). Thereafter, whatever may be the reasons and factors behind it, the public funds to develop state health services have declined drastically in the state. The data in Table 3.4 showed that there has been no appreciable increase in health infrastructure in Punjab since the mid-1980s.

Between the triennium period of 1978–79 to 1980–81 and the triennium period of 2002–03 to 2004–05, the total number of hospitals decreased from 244 to 219, the number of PHCs increased from 129 to 441, the number of dispensaries rose from 1,255 to 1,479, and of indigenous systems of medicine and homeopathy-related dispensaries from 454 to 636. Further, the proportion of rural hospitals just increased from 40.98 per cent during the triennium period of 1978–79 to 1980–81 to 43.77 per cent during the triennium period of 1984–85 to1986–87. Thereafter, the share of rural hospitals decreased consistently to 35.10 per cent during the triennium period of 1993.94 to 1995–96, and 33.33 per cent during the triennium period of 2002–03 to 2004–05. The proportion of rurally located dispensaries also showed a marginal decrease (from 85.31 per cent during the triennium period of 1978–79 to 1980–81 to 82.56 per cent during the triennium period of 2002–03 to 2004–05), despite the allocation of more central funds to rural health under the Minimum Needs Programme that has been implemented in India since the Fifth Five Year Plan (1974–79). This decrease in the proportion of rurally located dispensaries is perhaps due to the upgradation of many rural dispensaries into CHCs/PHCs in the same area during the period of 1984–2000 (Singh, 2005).

Further, the population served per institution also confirmed that there has been a very slow or no increase in the number of medical institutions owned by the state compared to the increase in the population of state. For instance, population served per hospital, which was 0.67 lakh during the triennium period of 1978–79 to 1980–81,

Table 3.4: Growth of Health Care Infrastructure in Punjab

Triennium Average	All Types of Institutions Allopathic					Non-Allopathic H & D	Population Served Per Institution Allopathic			Non-A	Population Served Per bed		
	H	PHC	D	CHCs	Total		H	D	Rural PHC*	H & D	Total	Rural	Urban
1978–79 to 1980–81	244 (40.98)	129 (81.65)	1255 (85.31)	- -	1630 (78.25)	454 (91.57)	0.67	0.13	1.13	0.36	854	1558	387
1981–82 to 1983–84	256 (43.43)	130 (85.38)	1742 (87.92)	- -	2137 (82.05)	533 (84.77)	0.68	0.10	1.13	0.33	802	1276	410
1984–85 to 1986–87	264 (43.43)	143 (86.51)	1779 (87.49)	- -	2187 (82.10)	563 (83.47)	0.70	0.10	1.06	0.33	811	1283	422
1987–88 to 1989–90	250 (42.72)	362 (93.38)	1564 (85.57)	23 (61.43)	2199 (81.74)	608 (83.20)	0.78	0.12	0.40	0.32	814	1291	436
1990–91 to 1992–93	210 (38.16)	441 (95.23)	1470 (84.06)	93 (60.79)	2213 (80.96)	628 (83.02)	0.98	0.14	0.34	0.33	841	1339	449
1993–94 to 1995–96	208 (35.10)	446 (94.62)	1465 (83.30)	104 (57.69)	2223 (79.86)	636 (79.87)	1.05	0.15	0.35	0.34	873	1408	477
1996–97 to 1998–99	208 (34.99)	444 (94.74)	1468 (83.04)	110 (58.36)	2229 (79.68)	635 (79.87)	1.16	0.16	0.37	0.38	954	1446	589
1999–2000 to 2001–03	216 (33.69)	441 (94.55)	1476 (82.70)	108 (60.99)	2240 (79.27)	635 (79.87)	1.13	0.16	0.39	0.38	957	1483.	566
2002–03 to 2004–05	219 (33.33)	441 (94.33)	1479 (82.56)	103 (62.14)	2242 (79.13)	636 (79.83)	1.17	0.17	0.40	0.40	1018	1555	624

Note: *Rural Population, Non-A means non-allopathic which includes Ayurvedic, Unani and Homeopathic.
H = Hospital, D = Dispensary, PHC = Primary Health Centres, CHC = Community Health Centres.
Figures in parentheses are percentage share of rural areas.
Source: Culled from *The Health Information of Punjab*, Directorate of Health and Family Welfare, Punjab, Chandigarh (Various Issues).

rose to 1.17 lakh during the triennium period of 2002–03 to 2004–05. In the case of PHCs that are exclusively for the rural areas, a different picture has emerged. Actually, due to the additional of many PHCs over the years, population served per PHC fell from 1.13 lakh persons during the triennium period of 1978–79 to 1980–81 to 0.34 lakh during the triennium period of 1986–87 to 1989–90, but rose to 0.40 lakh during the triennium period of 2002–03 to 2004–05 (Table 3.4). Consequently, at present, Punjab state is again away from the norms set by the Union Government in terms of population served per PHC (i.e. 30,000 populations per PHC). Thus, there was no increase in the number of PHCs/ CHCs in rural Punjab during the 1990s.

In economic theory related to public health services, it is the availability of beds per population and their utilization are considered to be the best indicators of the strength of facilities prevalent in the state. Since the utilization pattern of public health services has been attempted in the next section, the population served per bed has been attempted here. An assessment of the data on population served per bed reveals (Table 3.4) that population served per bed in rural areas did not show any improvement, as there was one bed for every 1,276 rural persons during the triennium period of 1981–82 to 1983–84 and that ratio rose to consistently to 1,555 persons per bed during the triennium period of 2002–03 to 2004–05. Also, population served per bed in urban areas also rose from 422 persons during the triennium period of 1981–82 to 1983–84 to 624 persons per bed during the triennium period of 2002–03 to 2004–05. This means that no appreciable effort was made by the government to improve upon the availability of more beds for indoor treatment in public-owned medical institutions of the state. In fact, the indoor treatment in these institutions has deteriorated during the post-reforms period of the study.

3.3.2 Partial Initiatives to Improve Quality of Health Infrastructure

The state government, despite being fully aware of these realities, has not made any planned effort/initiative to expand and bring reforms in the public health infrastructure, both in urban and rural areas since 1991. The only two initiatives, limited in scope, have been taken to reorganize state health department in Punjab. The **first initiative** is related to the corporatisation of public health services in the state by establishing the Punjab Health Systems Corporation (PHSC) during the late 1990s by taking over only 154 public hospitals ranging from district hospitals (17), sub-divisional hospitals (45) to CHCs /PHCs (92). The main motives of the PHSC are to: (i) upgrade the secondary health care system (on selective basis) and (ii) introduce the health reforms in the state health sector. This has been done with the help of World Bank Loan of Rs. 422 crore. This has generated a debate and created many suspicions in the minds of intellectuals, policy makers, and health employees, and also among the general public of the state. Many of them fear that it is the implementation of the IMF and World Bank's prescriptions of commercialization and corporatisation of health services in the state. Their doubts/ fears came true with the introduction of users' charges for every service provided by these institutions.

A part of services provided by the PHSC-owned institutions, by allowing the establishment of private diagnostic facilities at these institutions' premises, has been privatized, and the users' charges (high as well as comparable to the private sector in many cases) are being levied for every service provided by these hospitals. However, the government defence in setting up the PHSC rests on three counts: **One,** it will upgrade the secondary healthcare system in the state which is in bad shape and dire need of funds, with World Bank assistance; **Two,** the corporation will have inherent flexibility of taking decisions and it would be possible for the state to govern the employees better and to give various incentives/rewards to them on the basis of their performance; and **Three**, it will improve the utilization of public health services by attracting the patients on one hand, and generate internal funds at the institution level through users' charges for further improvement or expansion of health services on the other.

The **second initiative** related to improving health care in rural areas has been taken very recently, i.e. year 2006. Under this initiative, decentralization in the administrative control of health delivery system has been introduced, particularly in rural Punjab by handing over the control of 1,310 rural dispensaries to the district level PRIs (Zila Parishad). In this new dispensation, the service-providers (Qualified Doctor) are appointed on contract assignments. The concerned Zila Parishad has been allowed to appoint a service-provider @ rate of Rs. 3.50 lakh per year per dispensary. And, out of the Rs. 3.50 lakh contract money, the service-provider is responsible for hiring the services of one pharmacist, one peon and maintaining the basic sanitation and other facilities in the dispensary. At present, on an average, there is one government health dispensary for 10 villages and each is headed by a service-provider who works under the Zila Parishad. If the experience is successful, then the Punjab Health Department has promised to increase the rural dispensaries from 1,310 to 2,600 in the next year.

As per initial reports, this contract system is working well in the rural areas, the service-providers are available in the dispensaries to the rural patients during specified hours, the attendance is monitored by the village Panchayat and a ten-fold increase in patients has been recorded in the

OPDs of dispensaries. However, the critics point out that the administrative decentralization is no panacea for the ills of the health delivery system in the state, which requires appropriate public health interventions, state support and efficient personnel. For success of decentralization in the context of Punjab, it needs a process of devolution of powers, not just the delegation of responsibility by the state to the periphery. Actually, the former involves sharing of decision-making powers and control over the resources, not just the administrative decentralization or shifting the responsibility of resource mobilization, which often has a negative impact, especially on the poor living in the periphery (rural areas).

IV

3.4 Major Flaws in Public Health Services

As already reported, there was no major increase in government-owned health institutions in Punjab and beds in them since the 1990s. On the other hand, due to the collapse of administration and weak monitoring mechanism during the militancy period, the rent-seeking behaviour of most of health sector employees has become the hallmark of the health delivery system in the state. Now a days, due to the lack of state support and funds and reoriented priorities under the SAP of World Bank, the potentials of public health infrastructure, particularly in rural Punjab, have not been optimally utilized. In fact, the available health infrastructure was allowed to deteriorate during the time period of the1990s and onwards. Many studies looking into health services in Punjab have observed that there are glaring deficiencies in machinery, equipments, appliances, buildings and residential accommodation, etc. in public health institutions (Singh, 2005). Decentralization has not taken place and there is no community participation. The entire burden of critically ill patients falls on the private or corporate sector-owned hospitals. The district hospitals or hospitals attached with medical colleges in the state, which were the natural priority of such patients in the past, are not adequately funded, nor equipped with the latest technology/appliances and, therefore, not preferred by the rich and the middle class people as evidenced from the health care seeking behaviour of patients (Singh, 1991). Recent health policy changes introduced under the impact of globalization have, further, led to the withdrawal of government support of funds to public health sector and promoted private capital in the creation of provisions for health services in the state.

3.4.1 Low Utilization of Public Health Infrastructure

As per the economic theory of health care, bed occupancy ratio is considered to be a better indicator of utilization as well as strength of public health services, especially in the case of indoor treatment. The bed occupancy ratio in the state has, however, shown a dismal picture.

For example, district hospitals, which seem to be overcrowded with patients (bed occupancy ratio was around 100 per cent) between the year 1970 and the year 1985, have shown a downward trend in the bed occupancy ratio (Table 3.5). A sharper downward trend in bed occupancy ratio has been observed in the tehsil hospitals, hospitals exclusively for women and tuberculosis patients. The 30-bedded, 25-bedded and PHCs that are mostly located in rural areas have shown an abysmally low level of bed occupancy. Interestingly, 17 district hospitals taken over by the PHSC have not shown any impressive improvement in the bed occupancy ratio, as it was 58.1 per cent in the first half of 2001. Even hospitals attached with state medical colleges providing tertiary care in Punjab have witnessed a fall of about 50 per cent in bed occupancy, mainly due to

Table 3.5: Bed Occupancy Ratio in Punjab by Type of Hospital (selected years)

Year	Type of Hospital								
	District	**Tehsil**	**Women**	**T.B**	**50–Bedded**	**30–Bedded**	**25–Bedded**	**PHC**	**Whole State**
1980	97.4	79.5	79.9	82.2	–	–	–	–	–
1985	100.6	100.5	72.2	77.2	–	–	–	–	–
1990	91.6	65.7	37.3	74.3	50.8	16.3	R-26.5	20.5	63.9
1991	89.2	68.0	39.6	67.6	59.9	17.3	18.2	13.3	54.6
1992	82.5	77.4	42.4	61.8	66.5	17.0	12.0	21.7	65.8
1993	80.8	61.3	40.9	59.4	62.4	12.1	14.5	22.3	46.6
1994	84.6	62.8	38.4	55.6	60.3	14.7	16.7	18.3	48.3
1995	87.9	63.9	37.3	54.4	61.7	16.2	18.7	13.5	44.2
2000	69.0	For Hospital attached with Government Medical College, Patiala.							
2000+	50.0	For Hospital attached with Government Medical College, Amritsar.							
2000+	45.0	For Hospital attached with Government Medical College, Faridkot.							
2001	58.1	For District Hospitals owned by Punjab Health Systems Corporation.							

Source: 1. *Health Information of Punjab* (earlier Health Statistics Punjab), Directorate of Health and Family Welfare Punjab, Chandigarh (various issues).
2. *The Tribune*, 12 August, 2001.

the deterioration in quality care and introduction of user charges since May 1999. Consequently, patients who can afford medicare prefer to get them treated in private hospitals/nursing homes, which have grown by leaps and bounds in the state.

The existence of private sector-owned health services in Punjab is not a new phenomenon. The public-private mix has been existing for a long period, where the latter makes full use of the former, particularly with respect to supplying trained health persons (doctors, nurses, etc.) promoting health-related R&D and determining standards of treatment processes. Under global forces, a new phenomenon is the opening up of public domain health services to the private investment and introduction of high users' charges. Both these measures have, however, failed to augment health services for the poor or to bring about greater efficiency in the delivery of health services in the state. In fact, these measures have increased the cost of public health care so high that the poor patients are deprived of accessing the low or subsidized but quality care supposed to be provided by the publicly-owned health services.

In Punjab, private sector health clinics/hospitals have grown at a greater speed. And, among the private hospitals/ nursing homes in the state, many have better equipments and machinery than that of government hospitals. They have engaged specialists on contract basis and employed mostly untrained paramedical staff to deliver health care to the people. Moreover, with the advent of telemedicine, nuclear medicine, non-invasive and laparoscopic surgery techniques, the patients' first priority is the hospitals where these facilities are available on demand. That is why the corporate entrepreneurs (Ranbaxy, Oswal, Fortis, Escorts, etc.) are entering the health sector in a big way in urban Punjab, mainly to generate high profits. The Punjab Government is lending state support to them by providing land at concessional rates in the PUDA-developed urban colonies (Bhat, 2000).

Many micro-level studies also concluded that a large majority of people suffering from illness/disease preferred, instead of public sector institutions, private clinics for treatment even when they are unqualified/untrained (quacks). A study on the utilization pattern of health services in rural Punjab, based on the primary survey of 18 villages of Patiala District, reveals many interesting facts. The study highlights that about one-third of patients (32.78 per cent) used public health centres, and the remaining two-third (67.22 per cent) preferred private hospitals/nursing homes/ clinics for getting treatment (Table 3.6). With regard to

Table 3.6: Distribution of Patients who Preferred Treatment for Diseases/ Illnesses by Type of Health Institution

Type of Health	Patients Suffered from:		Total
	Chronic Diseases	Communicable and Other Diseases	
Public Sector			
Hospital	33 (17.74)	49 (8.28)	82 (10.54)
PHC/CHC/SHC	25 (13.44)	148 (25.00)	173 (22.24)
Sub Total	58 (31.18)	197 (33.28)	255 (32.78)
Private Sector			
Hospital/Nursing Home	8 (4.30)	3 (0.51)	11 (1.41)
Clinic	120 (64.52)	392 (66.22)	512 (65.81)
Of Which Unqualified	57 * (47.50)	207 * (52.81)	264 * (51.56)
Total	186 (100)	592 (100)	(778) (100)

Note: * It shows number of patients who opted for private clinics manned by unqualified (quacks) health personnel.
Figures in brackets are percentages
Source: *Singh (1991)*.

grading of public/private health facility, the data reveal two main trends. **One**, a small proportion of rural patients (10.54 per cent) received treatment in the government owned hospitals and more than one-fifth patients (22.24 per cent) got treatment from the government-owned CHC/PHC/SHC. **Two**, an overwhelming majority of patients (65.81 per cent) got treatment from the private clinics. Only 1.41 per cent patients preferred private hospitals or nursing homes to get treatment. Further, more than one-half patients who got treatment from private-owned clinics (51.56 per cent) actually got treated by unqualified health persons (called 'quacks' in popular parlance).

Another study reveals that in more than three-fifth surveyed villages (62 per cent) in Punjab, the rural respondents have reported easy access (near home) of public health facilities during the time period of survey. Interestingly, about one-fourth of households (24 per cent) used public health facility for treatment of minor ailments (cough, cold, fever, wounds, loose motion, etc.). In the case of major ailments (surgery, fractures, complicated deliveries, strokes, etc.), more than two-fifth households (42 per cent) preferred public health facility for treatment. Cheap treatment and easy access are the main causes for the villagers to show preference for the utilization of public health services. However, only a small proportion of households (less than 3 per cent) that makes use of public health institutions are fully satisfied with the service (Paul, et al., 2004). It means that the private health sector is the major reckoning force in the treatment of diseases/injuries in rural Punjab.

Further, the dismal picture of public health institutions can be gauged from the large number of sanctioned posts of doctors, paramedical staff and district-level health officers (on supervisory and monitoring duty) are lying vacant.

These sanctioned posts in Punjab's health department are deliberately kept vacant by imposing a ban on new recruitments, not due to the non-availability of qualified health personnel, but largely due to pressures of globally determined economic policy and resource crunch faced by the state. The data in Table 3.7 provide proof of the grim scenario. It revealed that about one-fifth of posts (18.68 per cent) in the health department of Punjab were lying vacant in 2005. Interestingly, one-sixth posts of medical officers (16.80 per cent) are also lying vacant, despite a large number of qualified doctors being unemployed and available for work in the state. Similarly, more than one-sixth of sectioned positions of paramedical staff (18.38 per cent) and about one-fourth of posts of drivers (22.93 per cent) have remained vacant. Indeed, it is true that more than one half of sanctioned post of the district-level health extension staff

Table 3.7: Position of Doctors, Paramedical Staff and District Extension Health Officers in Health Department of Punjab, 2005

Name of Post	Sanctioned	Filled Posts	Vacant Posts	Percentage of Vacant Posts
Medical Officers*	4,380	3,644	736	16.80
Paramedical Staff**	15,131	12,350	2,781	18.38
District Level Extension Health Officers/Supporting Staff***	278	121	157	56.47
Drivers	532	410	122	22.93
All Posts	20,321	16,525	3,796	18.68

Note: 1. * It means Medical Officers including Dental Doctors.
2. ** It includes Pharmacists, Ophthalmic Officers, Radiographers, Laboratory Technicians, Staff Nurses, Lady Health Visitors, Supervisors, ANMs, MPWs(M/F), etc.
3. *** It includes DMIEOs, District Drug Inspectors, Principal Tutors, Nursing Superintends, District Public Health Nurses, Food Inspectors, Block Extension Educators, Artist-cum-Photographer, etc.

Source: *Office of Director Health Services*, Department of Health and Family Welfare, Punjab, Chandigarh.

(56.47 per cent) that provide a crucial link to maintain quality checks in health-related fields remained vacant.

3.4.2 Non-Functional Rural Health Sector and Consequences

From the 1990s onwards, when globalization gained importance and became indispensable in India, the health sector reforms have also been introduced to bring about strategic but favourable changes in the health care delivery system. Under the health sector reforms, cutbacks in public welfare expenditure, donor-driven priorities, techno-centric public health interventions and increasing reliance on private sector in providing health care have become the hallmark of new health strategy (Qadeer, 2000). All these forces would not bring cheer to the illiterate, the poor, the downtrodden living in rural Punjab and the slum dwellers in urban Punjab. For instance, when cuts are imposed on public health expenditure, not only the secondary and tertiary care units are deprived of resources, but inevitably the CHC/PHC units also suffer immensely. And, when cutbacks in the social sector as a whole (education, rural development, social welfare and nutrition, etc.) and dwindling subsidies to the public distribution system (food rationing) are imposed, it means additional loss of inter-sectoral support to the people, especially the poor. In such a scenario, populations living at subsistence levels and below poverty line are becoming even more vulnerable. Some researches convincingly demonstrated that in rural areas, ill-health has become a major cause of indebtedness (Planning Commission, 1999).

A cursory look at Plan Documents of Punjab state has shown that already there are glaring deficiencies in the availability of machinery, equipments, appliances, buildings and residential accommodation, etc. in state-owned rural health institutions. In fact, there is little community participation in the health sector and decentralization at the village level has not taken place. In rural Punjab, the entire burden of health care (promotive, preventive and curative care) falls on rural CHCs/PHCs, which are not adequately equipped and not acceptable to the people, as evidenced by their health-seeking behaviour in case of illness/disease (Singh, 1991). Recent policy changes under the influence of globalization have further led to the withdrawal of government support of funds to the rural health sector. The distribution of rurally located health institutions by type and bed strength lent support to these conclusions (Table 3.8). The data reveal that a large majority of rural health institutions in Punjab (around 90 per cent) fell in 0–4 bedded category between 1986 and 2005. Further, there were 111 rural hospitals in 1986, and their number had decreased to 73 in 2005. Of these, more than four-fifth were of small size having a bed strength of 11–30 beds during 1985–2005 period. There is only one large-sized hospital at Beas (a rural location situated on the bank of River Beas) having 300 beds, but run by the Radha Swami Satsang, a philanthropist organization. One may thus safely conclude that an overwhelming majority of rural health centres are primarily consultation clinics. Hospitalization and emergency services (indoor treatment) are almost non-existent in these rural institutions. The data provided by the Chief Medical Officer (Civil Surgeon), Patiala District, revealed that in all rural PHCs and dispensaries located in Patiala district, no bed occupancy was reported during 2005–06. This finding could be true for all of rural Punjab. Thus, rural people are deprived of easily available, cost-effective and better quality treatment of public health services near their homes in rural areas of the state.

Further, the availability of government doctors and paramedical staff in rural health institutions is very much regressive. Although this could not be substantiated for want of aggregate data pertaining to the number of doctors and paramedical staff posted in the rural areas, yet the actual

Table 3.8: Distribution of Health Institutions in Punjab by Type and Bed Range

Bed Range	Year	Type of Health Institution							
		Hospital		CHC/PHC		Dispensary		Total	
		Rural	Urban	Rural	Urban	Rural	Urban	Rural	Urban
0–4	**1986**	–	6 (3.97)	50 (45.05)	7 (36.84)	1560 (99.36)	211 (95.48)	1610 (89.64)	229 (58.57)
	2005	2 (2.74)	8 (5.48)	379 (78.96)	18 (28.13)	1220 (99.92)	253 (98.06)	1601 (90.25)	279 (59.62)
5–10	**1986**	6 (5.22)	13 (8.61)	59 (53.15)	9 (47.37)	4 (0.25)	2 (0.90)	69 (3.84)	24 (6.14)
	2005	4 (5.48)	10 (6.85)	37 (7.71)	5 (7.81)	1 (0.08)	5 (1.94)	42 (2.37)	20 (47.27)
11–30	**1986**	102 (88.70)	53 (35.10)	2 (1.80)	3 (15.79)	6 (0.38)	8 (3.62)	110 (6.12)	64 (16.37)
	2005	58 (79.45)	39 (26.71)	63 (13.13)	38 (59.38)	–	–	121 (6.82)	77 (16.45)
31–50	**1986**	5 (4.35)	36 (23.84)	–	–	–	–	5 (0.28)	36 (9.21)
	2005	6 (8.22)	38 (26.03)	1 (0.21)	3 (4.69)	–	–	7 (0.39)	41 (8.76)
51–100	**1986**	1 (0.87)	24 (15.90)	–	–	–	–	1 (0.05)	24 (6.14)
	2005	2 (2.74)	25 (17.12)	–	–	–	–	2 (0.11)	25 (5.3)4
101 +	**1986**	1* (0.87)	19 (12.58)	–	–	–	–	1 (0.05)	19 (4.86)
	2005	1* (1.37)	26 (17.81)	–	–	–	–	1 (0.06)	26 (5.56)
Grand Total	**1986**	115 (100)	151 (100)	111 (100)	19 (100)	1570 (100)	221 (100)	1796 (100)	391 (100)
	2005	73 (100)	146 (100)	480 (100)	64 (100)	1221 (100)	258 (100)	1774 (100)	468 (100)

Note: * One 300-bedded Hospital in Rural Punjab. Figures in parentheses are percentages.
Source: *Culled from* ***Directory of Medical Institutions, Punjab***, Directorate of Health and Family Welfare Punjab, Chandigarh. (Various years)

position of these persons in 5 (Five) Development Blocks in Punjab state has highlighted that 21 posts of doctors (32.8 per cent) out of 64 sanctioned posts in these Blocks (Table 3.9) were lying vacant. Similarly, out of 123 sanctioned posts of paramedical staff, 22 posts (17.89 per cent) were lying vacant. As regards the availability of doctors and paramedical staff during the stipulated duty hours, the less said the better. Almost all the Block studies are unanimous in the large-scale absenteeism among the staff of these medical institutions under study. In many cases, the absenteeism was in connivance with the senior officers and patronage of other influential and well-connected persons who often reside in cities and towns. Apart from the problem of absenteeism, all the Block plan documents reveal: (a) poor and inadequate physical facilities, (b) non-availability of doctors round the clock; (c) non-availability of essential and basic medicines and lab test facilities; and (d) no arrangement for disaster management and emergency services in rural areas.

It is most deplorable that many of such non-existent facilities in public health facilities are no longer on the

Table 3.9: Position of Doctors and Paramedical Staff in Selected Development Blocks* in Punjab, 1998

Name of post	Total Sampled Institutions = RH-3, PHC-12, SHC-45 and SC-62	
	Sanctioned Posts	**Vacant Posts**
Doctor	64 (100.00)	21 (32.81)
Paramedical Staff	123 (100.00)	22 (17.89)

* Selected Development Blocks were Andana (District Sangrur), Malerkotla-1 (District Sangrur), Bathinda (District Bathinda), Machhiwara (District Ludhiana), and Saroya (District Nawa Shaher).

Note: RH—Rural Hospital, PHC—Primary Health Centre including Community Health Centre, SC—Sub-Centre.

Source: Singh S. (2005).

agenda of the Punjab government. As a consequence of a non-functional rural health infrastructure, the gaps in rural health facilities are being filled by the mushrooming growth of quacks in rural areas, who are playing havoc with the health of rural people, especially the poor, by charging exorbitantly high prices for sub-standard treatment and medicines. That is why a very wide gap still exists in rural and urban health indicators and infrastructure (Table 3.10). Although all the health indicators have shown positive development over the time period of study, the rural-urban differences are clearly visible. For instance, during the triennium period of 2002–03 to 2004–05, the birth rate in Rural Punjab was 21.6 per thousand live births compared to urban Punjab's birth rate of 18.0 per thousand live births. Similarly, the rural death rate was 7.3 per thousand compared to 6.1 per thousand in urban Punjab during the same period. As regards infant mortality rate, it was 53.7 per thousand live births and 38 per thousand live births in rural and urban Punjab respectively during the triennium period of 2002–03 to 2004–05 (Table 3.10). Similarly, the gap between populations served per bed is very wide in the state; as 1,555 persons and 624 persons were served per bed in rural and urban areas respectively (Table 3.4).

V

3.5 Concluding Remarks

The study clearly established that when the globalization process began to dominate in India, public investment in social sectors, especially in the public health sector in Punjab, was withdrawn, particularly during the decade of 1990s and onwards. Further, public health expenditure as a proportion of the NSDP in the state has remained less than 1 per cent for the most of years against the normative ratio of 3 per cent

Table 3.10: Birth Rate, Death Rate and Infant Mortality Rate by Location in Punjab

(Rate per thousand)

Triennium Period	Birth Rate			Death Rate			Infant Mortality Rate		
	Rural	Urban	Combined	Rural	Urban	Combined	Rural	Urban	Combined
1978–79 to 1980–81	29.8	27.6	29.3	10.4	8.0	9.9	105.0	72.7	96.0
1981–82 to 1983–84	30.8	28.7	30.3	9.8	6.9	9.1	84.7	57.7	78.7
1984–85 to 1986–87	29.6	27.8	29.1	9.5	6.3	8.7	75.3	47.0	68.0
1987–88 to 1989–90	29.1	27.5	28.4	8.8	7.0	8.3	66.0	55.7	63.3
1990–91 to 1992–93	28.4	25.2	27.5	8.6	6.0	7.9	61.3	42.0	50.0
1993–94 to 1995–96	26.6	21.8	25.3	8.3	5.9	7.6	59.0	37.7	54.0
1996–97 to 1998–99	24.6	18.9	23.1	8.0	6.2	7.5	55.7	39.3	52.3
1999–00 to 2001–03	22.4	18.6	21.4	7.7	6.1	7.3	56.0	38.0	52.3
2002–03 to 2004–05	21.6	18.0	20.7	7.3	6.1	7.0	53.7	34.3	49.7

Source: *Health Information of Punjab*, (various issues) Directorate of Health and Family Welfare, Government of Punjab, Chandigarh.

of the state/national income accepted in the country. Moreover, the dominant position of the central government in financing Punjab's planned health expenditure as well as in determining the state's health priority programmes has bad consequences (cutbacks in funds) for the more crucial 'public health and sanitation' programmes, which are more relevant for the state. Consequently, no visible expansion and improvements in the public health infrastructure both in rural and urban areas has been seen since 1991, except establishing the PHSC to upgrade secondary healthcare in the state. Still, very wide gaps are found in rural and urban health indicators in the state.

In Punjab, an overwhelming majority of public health infrastructure and services, due to lack of funds, faulty planning and poor governance, has become non functional and has shown a gross under-utilization pattern. Rural institutions continue to be starved of essential medicines, test facilities, first-aid kits, etc. and are primarily consultation clinics. Emergency and hospitalization services are almost non-existent in majority of these rural institutions. The rural people, especially the poor, are deprived of easily accessible, cost-effective and better quality treatment of public-owned health services near their homes.

The rich and emerging middle-income groups, who have become health conscious and have the capacity to pay, have begun to patronize private hospitals/nursing homes to get specialized treatment. In rural areas, the gap is being filled by the mushrooming growth of quacks that provide sub-standard medical treatment at exorbitantly high costs. The growing private health sector is largely unmonitored and unregulated, with no norms regarding quality or price of treatment. Even the new National Health Policy 2001 did not mention any of policy parameters in the fixation of charges and the standard of treatment provided by these private institutions. Further, inequities in income have resulted in differential access as well as utilization of health services in the state. These trends will seriously jeopardize the human resource development in the state and, subsequently, the formation of human capital, its improvement and maintenance and future economic growth in the state.

In a nutshell, globalization in the state has badly affected the working of public health institutions, favoured the role of private sector health services and implemented donor-driven priority programmes in the state. In the end, it is suggested that Punjab state should urgently take a long-range view of the health sector and integrate it with the other components rural development strategy. For this, state health policy should have the triple task of: (a) raising the demand for 'improved health'; (b) improving the quality of public health services; and (c) controlling the ever-growing reliance on the private health sector. Moreover, community participation (through PRIs and Local Bodies) should be enhanced in functioning and supervision of the whole public health system to make it more accountable to the users.

4

Agricultural Extension Services in Punjab

Agricultural research contributes to agricultural development in two ways: (a) it pushes yield barriers up through development of crop varieties, and (b) it develops agronomic and resource management practices for the specific varieties to perform optimally. Agricultural research brings new technology which contributes to economizing the production costs either by reducing costs directly or through increasing yield level. In both ways it contributes to increasing profitability, which is the most important driving force for effective use of research results. The lack of transmission of knowledge generated by the research system to the actual users (farmers) of research acts as a barrier for full utilization of potential of the research. The lack of effective research-extension linkages has been a perennial problem of the agriculture system in India. The main reason for this is that agriculture research and extension functions are conducted by independent organizations and there are less incentives to bring them together. Researchers consider extension as a less challenging activity, whereas there is no incentive for extension agents to establish close link with research institutions. The solution may be with diversification of institutional and funding base of the extension system, where all actors pool their resources and skills. The participation of private sector and voluntary organizations in extension system is of considerable importance for agricultural development.

The provision of information is an important function of extension. The information has to flow from researchers to farmers and from farmers to researchers. The involvement of farmers in the research extension system can be better ensured through involvement of farmers' organizations. The farmers have to be provided: (i) general information, such as prices of agricultural products and weather conditions, and (ii) specialized information, like scientific recommendations about soil tests, animal health, plant varieties, fertilizers and other chemical inputs, economic use of water, post-harvest technologies, marketing arrangements and resource management. The imparting of skills requires some personal contact with the farmer (Pal and Saxena, 2003).The extension workers and organizations can perform this task with more efficiency if they are able to inspire confidence among the farmers on the basis of their past performance. There are four models available for organizations of extension services. The first is called the *pure public sector model*. The extension in this model is planned, managed and funded by some public sector agency. The implementation is done by the designated agency as a public service. The second model is known as the *collaborative model*. The government and other agencies (such as producer organizations and service-providing NGOs) are jointly responsible for agreeing on priorities, models of operation, etc. The funding is generally made by the government but there is agreed division of responsibilities for implementation. The third model is known as the *contracting model of extension*. This is followed when there is a breakdown in the capacity of the government to plan and manage the system. Then the government contracts with private organizations and individuals to implement extension to agreed specifications.

The government staff is contracted in or partially funded by private agencies. The fourth model is known as *private sector model*. This is generally a commodity and area-based model of extension. This is managed, planned and funded by a private sector agency which recovers cost plus profit from the farmers. It is a kind of a service arranged by the private sector for which farmers have to pay for its use (Christoplos and Faruington, 2004).

Depending on the circumstances, a specific model is picked up by the government for implementation. Earlier the first model came into existence but in the recent period other alternatives are being tried in the country in different regions for different crops. In developing countries, extension service generates a large number of external economies such as rise in productivity, efficient use of scarce natural resources like water, land, soil fertility and preservation of environment and adequate production of foodgrains for food security. Besides, a large number of farmers are poor and belong to the category of small and marginal farmers. If public extension service is not available to farmers, they lose access to it because they can not afford to pay for this service. Consequently, productivity level remains very low, and the country may suffer on account of food security. While deciding about the source of funding and management of extension system, the principles of equity and efficiency have to be kept in mind. Besides, it is well known that fixed participations do not work in the tropical agriculture characterized by significant variations in agro-ecological and socio-economic conditions. Therefore, a dynamic extension model which combined training with field-based location specific research to provide farmers skills, knowledge and confidence to make ecologically sound and cost-effective decisions, seems more relevant. The farmers generally adopt technologies in a sequential manner, often accepting only a component of technology of increase over time. There are various socio-psychological characteristics such as age, education, farm size, mass media, extension participation, type of extension agency; risk orientation and training programmes exert considerable influence on the adoption of the new research system. There are better chances of adoption of new technologies if there is a farmer-centred extension and training programme. The existence of proper extension service enables farmers to adopt technologies quickly and increase the level of yield per acre.

An agricultural extension system provides a critical link between agricultural research and production in the fields. This link bridges the gap between per-hectare yields in the labs and actual yields at the farm level. An agricultural extension service actually transfers the technology from the labs to the farms. Several studies (Evenson and Jha, 1973; Feder et al., 1987; Evenson and Mckinsey, 1991; Kumar and Rosegrant, 1994) have established that the rates of return on agricultural research and extension are much higher than those realized from other investments in agriculture. The rates of return from the World Bank-funded project in irrigation were less than 10 per cent (Gulati et al., 1994). The rates of return on agricultural extension are considerably higher as the minimum rate of return in agricultural extension reported was 14 per cent by Evenson and Jha (1973) and the maximum rate of return reported was 177 per cent by Evenson and Mckinsey (1991). Agricultural extension services not only bridge yield gaps but help in adoption of new generation technologies and adaptation of these technologies to diverse production environments. At the same time, extension services can be useful in conservation of precious resources like soil and water and engagement of communities for collecting needs and rational utilization of common resources. Without effective extension services it is difficult to achieve sustainable development in agriculture (Pal and Singh, 1997). In view of the critical role of agricultural research and extension several committees (ICAR, 1988 and ICAR, 1995) have made recommendations to strengthen the national agricultural research and extension system. It is recommended that public funding be increased and private partnership be secured to strengthen the system and make it relevant.

The agricultural extension system in Punjab has emerged as a part of the agricultural extension system in India after Independence. India acknowledged the relevance of an agricultural extension service immediately after independence. The Community Development Project (CDP) and National Extension Service (NES) were launched respectively in 1952 and 1953. The purpose was to provide a number of services to rural areas in the field of agriculture, health and animal husbandry. The purpose of NES was to accelerate the pace of rural development. This includes increased employment and production through application of scientific methods in agriculture. Up to 1960, agricultural extension work was performed purely under guidance of state departments of agriculture (Sulaiman and Holt, 2004). This was also the case with Punjab state. The establishment of Punjab Agricultural University in 1962 led to its involvement in agricultural extension through the Directorate of Extension. The University initiated training programmes for officials and farmers. Programmes of demonstration and exhibitions were undertaken to take agricultural research to farmers in the villages to bridge gap between agricultural research and actual farm practices. The Indian Council of Agricultural Research (ICAR) became involved in the extension services with the National Demonstration Programme. The involvement of ICAR increased subsequently with establishment of Krishi Vigyan Kendras (KVKs), i.e. farm science centres.

Programmes such as Lab to Land Programme and the Operational Research Programme of ICAR were merged with KVKs. KVKs are funded by ICAR but work under the state agricultural universities. Thus, in Punjab, there are three public agencies involved in agricultural extension services, viz. (i) Department of Agriculture, Government of Punjab; (ii) Punjab Agricultural University, Ludhiana; and (iii) Indian Council of Agricultural Research (ICAR). Though there are three public agencies involved in the work of agricultural extension, yet funding sources are two. The Government of Punjab funds expenditure of the Department of Agriculture and is also the major funding source of Punjab Agricultural University, Ludhiana. The Government of India (GoI) provides funds through ICAR for KVKs in the state working under Punjab Agricultural University, Ludhiana.

Initiation and accomplishment of the Green Revolution in Punjab, to a large extent, can be attributed to the successful working of agricultural research and extension services in the state. The Government of Punjab provided adequate financial backing to the working of the system. Neither the Department of Agriculture of Punjab government nor the Punjab Agricultural University faced any financial crunch till the mid-1980s. The financial constraints for the system began to be experienced in the late 1980s and especially after 1991, when Government of India adopted the new economic policy. Under the new policy regime, the policy of fiscal discipline was adopted by emphasizing substantial reduction in government expenditure to bring down fiscal deficit. The state governments were encouraged to cut down their expenditure to keep fiscal deficit within limits. This had a visible affect on agriculture research and extension services in the state. The participation of the private sector in agricultural research and extension was envisaged (Planning Commission, 2002) as one of the alternatives to public sector involvement. This created a psychological environment that public funding need not be encouraged in agricultural research and extension. At the same time, it created an impression that public-funded agricultural research and extension have to emphasize improvement in efficiency rather than horizontal expansion. The new policy initiative led to a relative decline in flow of funds for agricultural research and development. In fact, the flow of funds for agricultural development had begun to decline in Punjab even before the new economic policy was launched in the country.

4.1 Public Expenditure on Agriculture and Allied Activities

The information presented in Table 4.1 brings out that around 9.83 per cent of the state budget on revenue account used to be allocated and spent for agriculture and allied activities between 1978–79 and 1980–81. This increased to 10.30 per cent during 1981–82 to 1983–84, but thereafter a relative decline of this budget started. This share of agriculture and allied services declined to 5.52 per cent of

Table 4.1: Level and Percentage Share of Public Expenditure on Agriculture and Allied Services in Punjab State's Budgetary Expenditure (Revenue Account)

(Figures in Rs. Crore at Constant Prices of 1993–94)

Triennium Average	Expenditure on Agriculture and Allied Services	Total State Expenditure	Percentage Share
1978–79 to 1980–81	149.41	1520.28	9.83
1981–82 to 1983–84	194.60	1889.60	10.30
1984–85 to 1986–87	179.49	2422.13	7.41
1987–88 to 1989–90	179.96	3100.12	5.80
1990–91 to 1992–93	227.76	4126.30	5.52
1993–94 to 1995–96	205.54	4761.69	4.32
1996–97 to 1998–99	204.15	5628.62	3.63
1999–00 to 2001–02	248.68	7125.86	3.49
2002–03 to 2004–05	270.20	9156.54	2.95

Source: *Statistical Abstract of Punjab*, ESO, Chandigarh (various Issues).

the budget during 1990–91 to 1992–93. This fall in the budgetary spending in agriculture happened during a period when the state was embroiled in terrorism. The priority of the administration had shifted from development to maintenance of law and order in the state. The budgetary allocations from development areas (including agriculture and allied activities) were shifted towards expenditure on police and security forces. The adoption of the new economic policy in 1991 further strengthened this tendency. Although normalcy began to be restored in the state from 1992 and by 1994 the state was completely free from the problem of terrorism, reduction in the relative share of expenditure in the agriculture and allied activities continued. The share of agriculture and allied activities in the state budget declined to 4.32 per cent during 1990–91 and 1992–93, which further declined to 3.63 per cent during 1996–97 to 1998–99. This fell in subsequent years and touched the lowest level of 2.95 per cent during 2002–03 to 2004–05. This is further confirmed by the information related to the number of sanctioned posts and filled posts in the Department of Agriculture, Punjab. The data prior to 1999–2000 related to filled posts is not available. Generally up to1992–93, the sanctioned posts were nearly filled. The number of sanctioned posts increased in the state from 1981–82 to 1992–93. The posts that were increased related to DDA (Deputy Director Agriculture), AO (Agricultural Officer), ADO (Agriculture Development Officer), and AI (Agricultural Inspector). The persons employed in these vacancies were mainly engaged in agricultural extension work. In the era of new economic policy, generally the number of sanctioned posts remained constant at 1,576 (only 3 vacancies of DDA were added from 2001–02 when the number of districts increased in the state). But the number of filled vacancies declined sharply. The number of sanctioned posts in 1999–2000 was 1,576, out of which 1,275 (80.90 per cent) posts were filled. In comparison to this, the number of sanctioned posts increased to 1,579 in 2005–06 and filled posts declined to 980 (62.06). As many as 90 posts of AO, 425 posts of ADO, all the 05 posts of AE, 5 posts of AE, 25 posts of AE (Gr. II) and 25 posts of AI are vacant and this rendered agricultural extension service of Department of Agriculture nearly paralyzed (Table 4.2).

4.2 Composition of Budget of Agriculture Departments

The capacity of the Department of Agriculture has further diminished, as revealed by the analysis of the budgetary expenditure of this sector (Table 4.3). In spite of the large number of posts being kept vacant, the proportion of salary component of budget of the department has increased from 17.24 per cent during 1981–82 to 1983–84 to 35.43 per cent during 2002–03 to 2004–05. The non-salary component has fallen from 82.76 per cent to 64.57 per cent during the corresponding period. This indicates the declining capacity of the staff to print new literature, organize demonstrative plots, test facilities at the agricultural laboratories and visit villages and also diminished resources to provide subsidies on new programmes such as introduction of new technologies in irrigation, new cropping patterns, new farm practices or installation of biogas plants (new sources of energy), etc. The salary budget witnessed a consistent increase even in the situation of diminishing number of persons mainly because of salary hikes. The non-salary budget recorded wider fluctuations from year to year indicating the ad hoc operations of the department.

4.3 Punjab Agricultural University (PAU)'s Extension Programmes

The position of Directorate of Extension of PAU is somewhat better than that of the Department of Agriculture. The staff position in agricultural extension presented in Table 4.4 reveals that the number of persons engaged in this activity

Table 4.2: Number of Sanctioned and Filled Posts of Agriculture Extension Staff, Department of Agriculture, Punjab, 1980–81 to 2005–06

YEAR	Administration Wing						Engineering Wing								Statistical Wing					
	DDA		AO		ADO		AE		AAE		AAE (Gr.II)		A.I. (Imp.)		SO		Assistant stat		TA	
	SP	FP	SP	FP	SP	FP	SP	FP	SP	FP	SP	FP	SP	FP	SP	FP	SP	FP	SP	FP
1981–82	39	N.A.	159	N.A.	920	N.A.	5	N.A.	17	N.A.	36	N.A.	25	N.A.	6	N.A	13	N.A.	33	N.A
1982–83	39	–	159	–	920	–	5	–	17	–	36	–	25	–	6	–	13	–	33	–
1983–84	39	–	159	–	920	–	5	–	17	–	36	–	25	–	6	–	13	–	33	–
1984–85	39	–	159	–	920	–	5	–	17	–	36	–	25	–	6	–	13	–	33	–
1985–86	39	–	159	–	920	–	5	–	17	–	36	–	25	–	6	–	13	–	33	–
1986–87	39	–	159	–	920	–	5	–	17	–	36	–	25	–	6	–	13	–	33	–
1987–88	40	–	217	–	1099	–	5	–	17	–	36	–	25	–	6	–	13	–	33	–
1988–89	40	–	217	–	1099	–	5	–	17	–	36	–	25	–	6	–	13	–	33	–
1989–90	40	–	217	–	1099	–	5	–	17	–	36	–	25	–	6	–	13	–	33	–
1990–91	40	–	217	–	1099	–	5	–	17	–	36	–	25	–	6	–	13	–	33	–
1991–92	41	–	217	–	1163	–	5	–	17	–	36	–	27	–	7	–	15	–	36	–
1992–93	44	–	221	–	1167	–	5	–	17	–	36	–	27	–	7	–	15	–	36	–
1993–94	44	–	221	–	1167	–	5	–	17	–	36	–	27	–	7	–	15	–	36	–
1994–95	44	–	221	–	1167	–	5	–	17	–	36	–	27	–	7	–	15	–	36	–
1995–96	44	–	221	–	1167	–	5	–	17	–	36	–	27	–	7	–	15	–	36	–
1996–97	45	–	221	–	1167	–	5	–	17	–	36	–	27	–	7	–	15	–	36	–
1997–98	45	–	221	–	1167	–	5	–	17	–	36	–	27	–	7	–	15	–	36	–
1998–99	45	–	221	–	1167	–	5	–	17	–	36	–	27	–	7	–	15	–	36	–
1999–00	45	30	221	194	1167	947	5	4	17	17	36	28	27	22	7	6	15	N.A.	36	27
2000–01	45	30	221	194	1167	947	5	4	17	17	36	28	27	22	7	6	15	–	36	27
2001–02	48	44	221	162	1167	967	5	4	17	12	36	28	27	22	7	5	15	–	36	32
2002–03	48	44	221	162	1167	887	5	4	17	12	36	28	27	22	7	5	15	–	36	32
2003–04	48	37	221	178	1167	767	5	4	17	9	36	28	27	18	7	5	15	–	36	23
2004–05	48	32	221	131	1167	742	5	4	17	8	36	28	27	17	7	5	15	–	36	33

Note: (I) SP-Sanctioned Posts, (II) FP-Filled Posts.
Source: *Office of Director of Agriculture*, Government of Punjab, Chandigarh.

Table 4.3: Salary and Non-Salary Component in Budget of Punjab Agriculture Department, Chandigarh

(Figures in Rs. Crore at 1993–94 Prices)

Triennium Average	Total Budget	Salary Component	% Share	Non–Salary Components	% Share
1981–82 to 1983–84	78.43	13.53	17.24	64.91	82.76
1984–85 to 1986–87	95.56	15.34	16.06	80.22	83.94
1987–88 to 1989–90	117.75	20.05	17.03	97.70	82.97
1990–91 to 1992–93	166.35	20.88	12.55	145.47	87.45
1993–94 to 1995–96	63.05	23.86	37.84	39.20	62.16
1996–97 to 1998–99	302.76	31.17	10.30	271.59	89.70
1999–00 to 2001–02	188.93	32.81	17.37	156.11	82.63
2002–03 to 2004–05	92.29	32.70	35.43	59.59	64.57

Source: *Directorate General*, Department of Agriculture, Chandigarh.

Table 4.4: Number of Posts for Agriculture Extension Services in PAU

Year	Status of Posts				
	Class-I	Class-II	Class-III	Class-IV	Total
1991–92	78	105	136	247	566
1992–93	72	130	183	276	661
1993–94	104	87	170	306	667
1994–95	132	120	203	356	811
1995–96	149	105	216	360	830
1996–97	157	108	228	376	869
1997–98	157	114	207	381	859
1998–99	161	123	186	397	867
1999–00	146	128	190	364	828
2000–01	154	127	185	385	851
2001–02	148	153	209	369	879
2002–03	146	148	206	378	878
2003–04	138	158	197	381	874
2004–05	135	133	171	381	820

Class-I Posts include Directors, Additional Directors, Associate Directors, Professors, and Assistant Professors.

Class-II Posts include Extension Specialists, Programme Coordinators, Agriculture Engineers, Readers, Lecturers, Scientists, Economists, and Physicists.

Class-III Posts include Assistants, Clerks/Senior Clerks/Junior Associates, Stenographers, Steno Typists, Production Assistants, Technical Assistants, Superintendents, Sub–Inspectors, Visitor Guides, Computer Operators, Editors, and Research Fellows.

Class-IV Posts include Foremen, Drivers, Electricians, Helpers, Beldars, Messenger Boys, Fieldsmen, Artists–cum–Photographers, Demonstrators, Chowkidars, Cooks, Malis, and Storekeepers.

Source: *Annual Budgets*, Punjab Agricultural University, Ludhiana (various issues).

increased from 566 in 1991–92 to 867 in 1998–99 and 879 in 2000–01, but declined to 820 in 2004–05. This is partly due to the ICAR-funded Krishi Vigyan Kendras (KVKs) scheme which led to establishment of eight new KVKs starting from 1991–92 to 1994–95 (Table 4.5). Each KVK is functioning effectively because all posts are filled. Along with five specialists, there is supporting staff in each KVK. Consequently, the number of staff in agricultural extension has been rising. But a number of posts that are funded by the Government of Punjab in the PAU are being kept vacant. The decision not to fill the posts falling vacant in the university has been mainly guided by and due to the reduced funding of Government of Punjab. This has led to a fall in the number of persons engaged in extension work, especially after the period of 2001–02.

The share of agricultural extension in the PAU budget has ranged between 8.44 per cent and 10.42 per cent during the last 25 years. The peak of this expenditure was reached during 1993–94 to 1995–96 when it reached 10.42 per cent of the total budget, which has fallen in subsequent years (Table 4.6). If expenditure on extension services funded by the ICAR is deducted (Table 4.5) from the total extension budget of PAU, then virtually the extension budget of PAU (at constant prices of 1993–94) has been stagnant after the period of 1990–91 to 1992–93. This indicates that although the budget of the university has increased by 68.11 per cent between 1991–92 to 1992–93 and 2002–03 to 2004–05, the GoP-funded budget for extension services has stagnated. This indicates the declining role of the state government in agricultural extension services.

The declining role of the public sector in agricultural extension could be expected to match the increased role of private sector. But this has not happened. The GoP launched a programme of crop diversification in the state in March

Table 4.5: Number of Krishi Vigyan Kendras (KVKs) with Starting Year and Their Estimated Budgets

(Figures in Million Rs.)

Year	Location of Krishi Vigyan Kendras (KVKs)									
	Gurdaspur (1982–83)	Ferozepur (1991–92)	Bathinda (1991–92)	Kapurthala (1991–92)	Hoshiarpur (1991–92)	Patiala (1991–92)	Langroya, Dist. Nawanshehar (1994–95)	Kheri, Dist. Sangrur (1994–95)	Faridkot (1994–95)	Total Estimated Budget (Million Rs.)
1991–92	0.80	–	–	–	–	–	–	–	–	0.80
1992–93	0.12	0.05	0.05	0.05	0.05	0.05	–	–	–	0.37
1993–94	0.86	1.08	0.98	0.96	0.97	0.97	–	–	–	5.82
1994–95	1.51	1.51	1.51	1.51	1.51	1.51	–	–	–	9.06
1995–96	1.05	1.05	1.05	1.05	1.05	1.05	2.65	2.65	2.65	14.25
1996–97	1.11	1.11	1.11	1.11	1.11	1.11	2.52	2.52	2.52	14.22
1997–98	2.39	2.26	2.66	2.26	2.26	2.26	1.93	1.93	1.93	19.88
1998–99	1.75	1.75	1.75	1.75	1.75	1.75	1.75	1.75	1.75	15.75
1999–00	1.95	1.95	1.95	1.95	1.95	1.95	1.95	1.95	1.95	17.55
2000–01	2.02	2.02	2.02	2.02	2.02	2.02	2.40	2.40	2.40	19.32
2001–02	2.02	2.73	3.84	3.00	3.93	2.18	3.00	2.65	2.04	25.39
2002–03	3.52	2.66	4.25	3.2	3.94	3.00	3.06	3.00	3.00	29.63
2003–04	3.62	3.07	4.80	3.43	3.18	3.56	3.05	3.05	3.20	30.95
2004–05	3.60	3.28	4.23	3.56	3.21	3.4	4.31	4.2	3.91	33.70

Note: Figures in parentheses are the starting year of the KVKs.
Source: *Annual Budgets*, Punjab Agricultural University, Ludhiana (various issues).

Table 4.6: Total Expenditure, Expenditure on Extension Services and Percentage Share of Extension Services in PAU

(Rs. Crore at Constant Prices of 1993–94)

Triennium Average	Total Expenditure	Expenditure on Extension Services	Percentage Share of Extension Services
1981–82*	33.37	2.93	8.78
1986–87*	44.01	3.73	8.48
1987–88 to 1989–90	47.52	4.01	8.44
1990–91 to 1992–93	51.46	4.84	9.40
1993–94 to 1995–96	52.87	5.51	10.42
1996–97 to 1998–99	62.30	5.82	9.33
1999–00 to 2001–02	76.53	6.82	8.91
2002–03 to 2004–05	86.51	8.28	9.57

Note: *Information for other years was not available.

Source: *Annual Budgets*, Punjab Agricultural University, Ludhiana (various issues).

2003. A serious attempt was made to involve private companies like Advanta India Limited, Proagro Seed Co. (Pvt.) Ltd., Sygenta India Ltd., United Breweries Ltd., Pioneer India Ltd., Indian Glycols Ltd., Mahindra Shubh Labh Ltd., Tata Rallies India Ltd. and Reliance India Ltd. These companies got involved in seed trading and trading of the produce, but did not set up their agriculture research and extension centres. This led to a bitter experience of the farmers with these companies and they decided to distance themselves from contract farming as these companies failed to provide any extension service (Gill 2004; and Dhaliwal et al., 2004). One of the factors for failure of the diversification programme of the GoP has been weak/non-existent extension service for new proposed crops. The per-acre yields of major crops in the state, like foodgrains, sugar-cane and cotton, are either stagnating or showing a negative growth rate. The government is unable to change the cropping pattern and introduce new varieties because the public sector agricultural extension has collapsed and the private extension has not come into existence, leading to a pathetic situation for farming and farmers.

5

Summary, Conclusions and Policy Recommendations

Globalization is referred to as a strategy of economic development where borders of countries do not matter for movement of commodities, services, capital, finance, technology and information. This generates a process of economic integration and growing inter-dependence between countries of the world economy. The first strong wave of globalization took place during 1870 to 1914, when it was stopped by the First World War. This wave was shaped by colonialism and was dominated by imperialist countries which occupied colonies and established colonial empires. Great Britain emerged as the most powerful country in the world and Pound Sterling mediated most of the global transactions under the gold standard currency system. The colonies were in a subordinate position to the requirements of imperial powers and were controlled through superior military force. The end of colonialism after the Second World War led to political independence of the colonies and the newly independent countries adopted a development strategy which consciously attempted limited openness and integration with the global economy. Most of the ex-colonial countries attempted autonomous development and a self-reliant economy with the active role of the government in the development affairs. This was a departure from the colonial era, which was characterized by open economies and unregulated activities. The role of the state was enhanced for industrialization with a large component of import-substitution where local producers enjoyed protected market.

This strategy, however, began to face internal and external challenges in the 1980s. Internally, several economies faced slow growth rates with low levels of efficiency caused by bureaucratic delays and associated corruption. The external challenge came from the IMF, the World Bank and the U.S. Treasury in the form of the Washington Consensus. This got a lot of support from the MNCs and media under their control. The strategy of development under the Washington Consensus constituted privatization (reducing the role of public enterprises) liberalization (freeing markets from controls and regulations), macro stability (reduction in public spending) and globalization (removal of barriers in the movement of commodities, finance and capital). The meltdown of the Soviet Bloc and the formation of WTO gave a big boost to the present wave of globalization.

In the post-Second World War period, the nation-state became a symbol and repository of sovereignty of a nation. It became an ultimate source of authority and arbiter of disputes among people. The state became engaged in economic stability (management of effective demand), economic growth (capital accumulation) and the provider of welfare activities at concessional rates, especially in health, education, agricultural extension, and provision of public utilities, creating an image of cooperative capitalism in developed countries. This was also replicated in the developing countries. This generated a tendency of an internal orientation to economic nationalism by focusing on internal market and welfare activities. The Cold War contributed to this process indirectly and the threat of socialism acted as a cementing factor to ideologically unite the capitalist market economies. Though there was variation in the degree of the role of the state in various countries, the direction was the same.

The new phase of the globalization which began in the 1980s has been accompanied by gradual erosion in the role of the state. There has been a paradigm shift in development strategy from state-centric to market-centric. The consolidation of MNCs in production of goods and services, phenomenal increase in international financial flows, emergence of information and communication technology and formation of the WTO along with the IMF and the World Bank contributed in big way to the erosion of the role of the state. The Indian economy faced a paradigm shift in the development strategy.

India adopted neo-liberal strategy in 1991 in the wake of serious balance of payment crisis which the country faced then. Far-reaching changes were introduced in major sectors of the economy. This included free entry and exit through delicensing, removal of MRTP Act and Foreign Exchange Regulation Act (FERA), privatization of public enterprises, opening up of health, education, insurance, banking, infrastructure, roads, and air transport services to the private sector. The economy has been opened up to outside world both in trade of goods and services and for investment by the MNCs. In an effort to achieve fiscal stabilization, there has been shrinkage in the role of government in running and management of the economy. The government withdrawal has been visible in the area of electricity, oil and natural gas, banking and insurance sector, agricultural research and extension, health and education services.

India is a large country which is territorially organized into 35 units consisting of 28 states and seven union territories. Depending on the specific situation, the impact of neo-liberal policy on the role of state is not equally experienced in all the states and the union territories. The Punjab region is one of the most advanced states in India. The prosperity of the state has been the outcome of the Green Revolution ushered in the mid-1960s. This has been the result of pro-active state intervention through massive public investment in irrigation, rural electrification, rural link roads, agricultural marketing infrastructure, network of credit institutions, agricultural research and extension. This was also accompanied by large expansion of health and education under public provisioning of these services. This led to rural development and the dairy development programme kickstarted the on-farm and off-farm economic activities in the state. The process of agriculture industry linkage also began to emerge through the government intervention.

But this process of development faced a big shock when the Punjab state was engulfed by militancy-related violence during the time period 1982–1992. This led to a change in orientation of administration from development administration to law and order oriented administration. In Punjab, the long spells of President's Rule under the bureaucracy led to degeneration of governance, thereby seriously impairing the financial health of the state with the collapse of tax collection machinery. When the state recovered from militancy and normalcy was restored, the capacity of government to intervene for correction of distortions in the development had become negligible. This is evident from the declining share of public expenditure for investment in social and economic sectors. This share has continuously declined from 72.98 per cent of the total public spending during the triennium ending 1980–81 to 41.05 per cent during the triennium ending 2004–05. This was in spite of the fast decline in annual growth rate of the economy, rising unemployment, deterioration in health standards and collapse of education, especially in the rural areas.

Faced with a severe financial crisis and declining capacity of the state to collect tax as a percentage of state domestic product (SDP), the successive governments resorted to massive public borrowings, inviting very high interest and debt payment services reaching a peak of 52.05 per cent of total non-development expenditure in the triennium ending 1998–99. Another component accounting for major share has been the pensions and miscellaneous services reaching a peak of 40.79 per cent of the total non development spending in the state in the triennium ending 2004–05. Faced with the problem of militancy, the expenditure on police and security could not be controlled; therefore, cuts in public funds were applied on the soft targets like health, education, agricultural extension services, etc. Thus, Punjab state experienced an early and massive withdrawal of the government from the development activities and in the social sectors like education, health and agricultural extension services compared to the surrounding states like the Haryana, Himachal Pradesh, Rajasthan, and Jammu and Kashmir.

The study convincingly pointed out that the state's withdrawal from social sectors (education and health services) and other development activities (agricultural extension services) began in the mid-1980s, when Punjab was embroiled in civil strife (created by the terrorist violence) and resultant law and order problem. However, even after the return of normalcy in Punjab (1992), state withdrawal continued because of the adoption of neo-liberal stabilization policy regime at the national-level (1991). The thrust of this macro stabilization policy, characterized as liberalization, privatization and globalization (LPG), focused on the fiscal consolidation and reduction of subsidies in the state. The Punjab state implemented this more rigorously as it faced an acute financial crunch (GoP, 2002). Faced with a large fiscal deficit, the state government resorted to withdrawal of budgetary support to the education, health and agriculture (including extension services) sectors. This is evident from the falling share of funds allocated to these sectors out of the total budgetary expenditure of Punjab government during the last 25 years.

This fall in state budgetary support was accompanied by the implementation of pay revision of employees in wake of the recommendations of the Fifth Pay Commission (1996) during 1998–99. The increased salary bills led to a fall in the capacity of these sectors to sustain their activities effectively. The government resorted to the policy of keeping a large number of posts vacant in these departments. The reduced budgetary support and falling number of employees crippled the capacity of public sector institutions to perform the functions assigned to them effectively. This was also accompanied by a decline in the monitoring and supervisory roles in these departments. The delayed promotions and lack of funds for field/supervision work weakened the monitoring and supervision of the field staff. Besides, the orientation of administration, which was transformed from that of 'developmental and public service' to the maintenance of law and order during the disturbed decade (1982–1992), has not yet been rectified. This has generated apathy in administration towards social sectors and development. It has made public sector institutions ineffective in providing education and health in the rural area, and public sector agricultural extension service have become fragile.

The vacuum created by the weakening of public sector institutions in education, health and agricultural research began to be filled by the private sector schools (unaided), private hospitals/nursing homes (many claim to have Five Star Status), and private companies like the MNCs. The private sector institutions being run with sole motive of profit, have been charging very high tuition fees in the private schools, consultation/treatment fees in the hospitals and clinics, and very high charges for clinical tests and indoor treatment. This has led to exclusion of a large section of population from accessing health and education services provided in the private institutions. With deterioration of quality of education and health services provided in the public sector institutions, and collapse of public health services and the non-affordability of private sector services, the weaker sections of society, especially children belonging to the Scheduled Castes, low-paid workers and poor peasants are being denied these services in the state.

In the education sector of the state, there has been a rapid growth of unrecognized privately financed primary schools during the last decade or so. These schools have begun to attract an increasing proportion of students. The proportion of students enrolled in these unrecognized private schools at the primary level has been reached to 24.50 per cent in 2000–01 from 20.34 per cent in 1995–96. The infrastructural facilities are lacking in the schools of the state. On the whole, there are 1,153 schools (6.18 per cent) without their own buildings, 6,761 schools (36.23 per cent) without a boundary wall, 7,976 schools (42.74 per cent) without playgrounds and 13,179 schools (70.62 per cent) without the facility of toilets for children.

The constrained supply of public resources and unregulated entry and functioning of private players has serious implications in terms of educational participation and outcomes. The total number of students in elementary stage declined from 29.93 lakh (1991) to 29.43 lakh (2004). Noticeably, their number increased in absolute sense in 1991

(29.93 lakh) over 1981 (27.10 lakh). The data also show that the number and proportion of students belonging to Scheduled Castes improved. Interestingly, their proportion (39.57 per cent) overall has gone up more than that of their share in population of the state, i.e. 28.90 per cent in 2001. In this context, it is to be noted that it has been the outcome of shifting of their wards, by those parents who could afford good private education, from the government schools in favour of the private ones. The overall literacy rate in the state increased from 48.10 per cent in 1981, to 58.51 per cent in 1991, and to 69.95 per cent in 2001. But, in 2001, about 30 per cent of the population in the literacy-eligible-category (six years and above) was illiterate. During the period of two decades (i.e. 1981 to 2001), the literacy rate recorded 1.89 per cent annual compound growth rate. Moreover, the growth in literacy rate slowed down during the decade 1991–2001 (i.e. 1.77 per cent) more than that of the decade1981–1991 (i.e. 1.98 per cent). It seems that until and unless adequate measures are taken, it would take a considerable number of years for the state to eradicate illiteracy. Further, the educational progress in the state is highly iniquitous in terms of regions, districts, locations, sexes and population groups. Male literacy in 2001 was 75.63 per cent and female 63.55 per cent. Urban literacy stood at 79.10 per cent and rural literacy at 64.70 per cent in 2001. Interestingly, in all literacy categories, the growth rate declined in the1990s as compared to the 1980s.

The drastic change in the education sector in the state occurred when the share of students' population is viewed in general population. The share of student population in general population declined from 19.86 per cent in TE (1980–81) to 16.89 per cent in TE (2001–02). During the corresponding years, the proportion of elementary education-level students declined from 17.38 per cent to 12.56 per cent, i.e. 4.82 percentage points. The educational outcomes turned out to be highly disturbing, such as high dropout rates, poor pass percentages, and presence of overage children. Moreover, in the reform period, these outcomes deteriorated further, like the percentage of successfully passed outs students declined from 65.96 per cent in 1998 to 49.18 per cent in 2001–03 in the case of regularly appeared students in matriculation examinations. Similarly, dropout rates reached 48.10 per cent in 2002–03 from the first to tenth standard. Furthermore, for the upper-primary level, the percentage share of overage children was 18.19 per cent in 2004–2005. There are also indications that the educational attainments of poor households fell during 1992–93 and 1998–99 across all the grades from first to nine. For example, as many as 75 per cent of children from the top quintile households completed the 9th grade in 1998–99, compared to only 9 per cent of children from the bottom quintile households who reached the same level of grade.

Another serious problem of the education sector of the state is the growing exclusion of rural students from university-based education. This has emerged from the recent survey report prepared by the Punjabi University, Patiala. The report shows that during the academic session 2005–06, the proportion of rural students in the Universities of Punjab state and their Regional Centres was just 4.07 per cent (911 rural students out of 22,360 total students). The share of rural boys and rural girls in universities was 4.96 per cent and 3.06 per cent, respectively. The perusal of data shows that the share of education sector as such in the state budgetary expenditure declined considerably over the study period of twenty-four years, i.e. 1978–79 to 2001–02. In terms of average of triennium of financial years, it declined from 23.66 per cent in 1978–81 to 16.82 per cent in 1999–02.

The education expenditure (overall) on per-student basis experienced the real growth rate of 5.99 per cent per annum during first sub period (i.e. 1978–79 to 1989–90), which declined to 5.55 per cent during second sub-period (i.e. 1990–91 to 2001–02). The share of plan component was very low in case of all categories as well as overall level of education. During the study period, i.e. T.E. (1980–81) to T.E. (2001–02), the share of Plan component remained very low. It declined to its lowest level (3.85 per cent) in T.E. (1986–87), and rose to 12.32 per cent during T.E. (2001–02) in the case of overall education budget. The non-Plan expenditure constituted 87.68 per cent of education budget during T.E. (2001–02). The Plan-expenditure during the decade of the 1990s, on an average, was higher than that of the 1980s. Per-student expenditure at current prices witnessed a rise consistently. It rose from Rs. 346.99 during T.E. (1980–81), to Rs. 1,173.03 during T.E. (1989–90), and ultimately to Rs. 4,755.19 during T.E. (2001–02). Further, the per-student expenditure was found to be lowest in case of elementary education than those of the other categories.

Regarding the status of health services, the study clearly established that, when the process of globalization began to dominate in India, public investment in the public health sector in Punjab was slowly withdrawn, particularly during the 1990s and onwards. Public health expenditure as a proportion of the NSDP in the state has decreased to less than 1 per cent during the last decade, compared to the normative ratio of 3 per cent at the national-level. Moreover, the dominant position of the central government in financing Punjab's planned health expenditure as well as in determining the state's health priority programmes has bad consequences (cutbacks in funds) for the more crucial 'public health and sanitation' programmes, which are more significant and relevant for the state. Due to lack of state support, no visible expansion and improvements in the public health infrastructure in rural and urban areas has been observed since 1991, except establishing the PHSC with World Bank aid (donor-driven priority) only to upgrade secondary healthcare institutions. There are still wider gaps in rural and urban health indicators in the state.

In Punjab, an overwhelming majority of public health infrastructure and services, due to lack of funds, faulty planning and poor governance, has become non functional and has shown gross under-utilization pattern. Rural institutions continue to be starved of essential medicines, test facilities, first aid kits, etc. and are primarily consultation clinics. Emergency and hospitalization services are almost non-existent in majority of these rural institutions. The rural people, especially the poor, are deprived of easily accessible, cost-effective and better quality treatment of public-owned health services near their homes.

The rich and emerging middle-income groups have begun to patronize private hospitals/nursing homes in the name of getting specialized treatment. Consequently, a large number of big hospitals are being opened in urban Punjab. In the rural areas, there is a mushrooming growth of unqualified doctors (quacks) who provide sub-standard medical treatment at exorbitantly high costs. The growing private health sector is largely unmonitored and unregulated, with no norms with regard to quality or price of treatment. Even the latest National Health Policy 2001 did not mention any of policy parameters in the fixation of charges and the standard of treatment in the private health institutions. In a nutshell, the working and quality of public health institutions in the era of globalization have deteriorated. The state has begun to favour the private sector-owned health services and donor-driven priority programmes.

In the agriculture sector, the share of agriculture and allied activities in the state budget declined from 9.83 per cent during the T.E.1980–81 to 4.32 per cent during the T.E.1992–93, which further declined 3.63 per cent during the T.E.1998–99. This has fallen in the subsequent years and touched the lowest level of 2.95 per cent during the T.E. 2004–05. Moreover, the capacity of Department of Agriculture in extension services has further diminished, as revealed by the analysis of the budgetary expenditure to this sector. In spite of the large number of posts being kept vacant, the proportion of salary component of budget of the Department of Agriculture increased from 17.24 per cent during the T.E.1983–84 to 35.43 per cent during the T.E. 2004–05. The non-salary component has fallen from 82.76 per cent to 64.57 per cent during the corresponding period.

The withdrawal of the public sector agricultural extension services has deprived the farming sector and farmers of the expert advice on the quality and quantity of agriculture inputs, their timely use, efficient use and conservation of water and soil, adoption of new seeds and technologies, sustainable cropping pattern or mix of farm and off-farm economic activities. The private sector has not stepped in to fill this gap in spite of the efforts of the government. This has created a crisis-like situation in the agriculture sector of Punjab. The productivity levels of major crops are either declining or stagnating and no viable alternatives to the existing cropping pattern are accessible to the majority of the farmers.

Specific Public Policy Recommendations

The society and economy of Punjab state require strengthening of the public sector institutions so that they provide social services to the common persons at affordable rates and play a developmental role. At the same time, the efficient and effective functioning of public sector institutions is necessary to provide healthy competition to the private service providers so that they do not indulge in fraudulent practices and exploit the common people by resorting to cartels/monopolies and charge for these services at exorbitant rates unconnected to the costs of the service/s. In view of the above, several policy recommendations emerge from the analysis:

1. Education and health are vital social sectors of the state. Since the state has no mineral base except fertile soil and water resources, the future of Punjab depends upon building and developing its human resource base. This cannot be done without strengthening the health and education sectors in the state. At present, the major part of these services is being provided by the public sector institutions, which are in bad shape. There is an urgent and immediate need to restore budgetary support to education and health, at least on a par with the triennium ending 1980–81.
2. The depletion of staff due to retirement needs to be replaced and increased in critical areas. A blanket ban on recruitment for nearly a decade (more effectively for the last five years) speaks volumes about the apathy of administration and power in the province. This unwise policy needs to be replaced by a more practical policy of recruiting adequate number of personnel necessary for managing these sectors.
3. Monitoring and regulatory mechanisms need to be made effective so that public sector institutions, their infrastructure and personnel function effectively and in a transparent manner. Adequate provisions for funds and other resources need to be made available for supervision of the field staff. IT services can be installed to economize the monitoring mechanism.
4. Agricultural extension services are a critical link between agricultural research in the labs and the

farming practices of the farmers. They need to be restored through adequate budgetary support and recruitment of qualified staff to guide the farming community in the state. The second Green Revolution in the province will remain a mirage without proper public sector agricultural extension services as the experiences of the last decade show that the private sector is unable to fill the gap created by public sector extension services. Earlier, the Pepsi experiment failed in early 1990s and the recent experience of involving several private sector companies in 2003 has not shown positive results either. This imparts a lesson that profit-oriented organizations would never be able to provide effective merit good services to the majority of the farmers. The agricultural extension services must be put in the top place to bring Punjab agriculture out of crisis and prepare it for a second Green Revolution.

5. The experience of the working of private sector organizations reveals several limitations in their working in social sectors like education, health and development-oriented agricultural extension services. They resort to fraudulent practices when people are made to pay high charges for poor quality of service and there is no link between the rates charged and cost of services. Sometimes people are misguided by private institutions in providing services, especially in health and agricultural extension services. This leads to fatal losses and adds to agony of the people. Therefore, it is of utmost importance to introduce a strong regulatory mechanism for private institutions in social sectors and developmental extension services. This regulatory mechanism must fix the charges for various services; check fraudulent practices and ensure

that these institutions conform to the norms of social policy so that they are accessible to weaker sections.

6. In order to introduce a healthy competition between public and private institutions, it should be obligatory for private institutions to be equally involved in fulfilment of social goals in the areas such as health, education and agricultural development extension services.

Bibliography

Ahluwalia, I.J. and I.M.D. Little (1998), *India's Economic Reforms and Development: Essays for Manmohan Singh*, Oxford University Press, New Delhi.

Amin, S. (1974), *'Accumulation on World Scale'*, 2 vols., *Monthly Review Press*, New York.

Baran, Paul (1958), 'Political Economy of Backwardness', in Aggarwal A.N. and Singh S.P. (eds.), *Economics of Underdevelopment*, Oxford University Press, New Delhi.

Baru, R. (1998), *Private Health Care in India: Social Characteristics and Trends*, Sage Publications, New Delhi.

Baum, F. (2001), 'Health, Equity, Justice and Globalization: Some Lessons from People's Health Assembly', *Journal of Epidemiology and Community Health*, Vol. 55, No. 9, pp.613-616.

Bhaduri, A. (2002), 'Nationalism and Economic Policy in the Era of Globalization', in Deepak Nayyar (ed.), *Governing Globalization: Issues and Institutions*, Oxford University Press, New Delhi.

Bhaduri, A. and Deepak Nayyar (1996), *The Intelligent Person's Guide to Liberalization*, Penguin Books, New Delhi.

Bhalla, G.S. (1994) (ed.), *Economic Liberalization and Indian Agriculture*, ISID-FAO, New Delhi.

Bhat, R. (2000), 'Issues in Health: Public-Private Partnership', *Economic and Political Weekly*, Vol. 35, No. 52 and 53, pp. 4706–16.

Brar, J. S. (2002), 'Basic Education, Health Care and Economic Growth in Punjab: Achievements, Gaps and Imbalances', *Man and Development*, Vol. 24, No. 1, pp.51–63.

Brar, J.S., Sukhwinder Singh and R.S. Ghuman (2008), 'Costs of Higher Education in Punjab: Level, Patterns and Emerging Issues', *Journal of Educational Planning and Administration,* Vol. XXII, No. 2, pp.153–177.

Chadha, G.K. (2004), 'Human Capital Base of the Labour Force: Identifying Worry Spots', *The Indian Journal of Labour Economics,* Vol. 47, No. 1, pp.3–38.

Chatterjee, P. (2007), 'Child Malnutrition Rises in India despite Economic Boom', *The Lancet,* Vol. 369, 28 April, pp.1417–1418.

Christoplos, I. and J. Faruington (2004) (eds.), *Poverty, Vulnerability, and Agricultural Extension-Policy Reforms in Globalizing World,* Oxford University Press, New Delhi.

Cornia, G. A. (2001), 'Globalization and Health: (a) Results and Options', *Bulletin of World Health Organisation,* Vol. 79, No. 9, Economics of Health and Medical Care. Macmillan and Co, London.

Dhaliwal, H.S., Manjit Kaur and Joginder Singh (2004), *Evaluation of Contract Farming Scheme in the Punjab State,* Mimeo, Department of Economics, PAU, Ludhiana.

Dreze, J. and A. Sen (1995), *India: Economic Development and Social Opportunity,* Oxford University Press, U.K.

EPW (2003), *'Current Statistics, Foreign Investment Approval and Actuals: A Profile', Economic and Political Weekly,* Vol. 38, No.43, p.4499.

Evenson, R. E., and D. Jha (1973), 'The Contribution of Agricultural Research System and Agricultural Production in India', *Indian Journal of Agricultural Economics,* Vol. 28, No. 4, pp.212–230.

Evenson, R.E. and J.W. Mckinsey (1991), 'Research, extension, infrastructure and productivity change in Indian Agriculture', in R.E. Evenson and C.E. Pray (eds.), *Research and Productivity in Asian Agriculture,* Cornell University Press, Ithaca and London.

Feder, G., L. Laus and R.H. Slade (1987), 'Does Agricultural Extension Pay? The training and visit system in northwest India', *American Journal of Agricultural Economics,* Vol. 69, pp.677–686.

Felix, David (1998), 'Asia and Crisis of Financial Globalization', in D. Baker, G. Epstein and Robert Pollin (eds.) *Globalization and Progressive Economic Policies,* Cambridge University Press, Cambridge.

Frank, A. G. (1975), *On Capitalist Underdevelopment,* Oxford University Press, New Delhi.

GATT Agreements 1994, (1995), World Trade Centre (WTC), Bombay.

Ghuman, R.S., Sukhwinder Singh and J.S. Brar (2009); *Professional Education in Punjab: Exclusion of Rural Students,* Publication Bureau, Punjabi University, Patiala.

Gill, S. S. and R. S. Ghuman (2000), 'Punjab, Rural Health-Proactive Role for the State', *Economic and Political Weekly,* Vol. 35, No. 51, pp.4474–7.

Gill, S.S., Sukhwinder Singh and J.S. Brar (2005), *Financing of Secondary Education: Grants-in-Aid Policies and Practices in Punjab,* A Report submitted to NIEPA, New Delhi.

Gill, S. S. (2004), 'Contract Farming Hurts Farmers', *The Tribune,* 17 September, 2004, Chandigarh.

Government of Punjab (2002), *White Paper on the State's Finances,* Department of Finance, Government of Punjab, Chandigarh.

Government of India (1992), *Eighth Five Year Plan 1992–1997,* Planning Commission, Government of India, New Delhi.

Grosh, M. and P. Glewwe (2000), *Designing Household Survey Questionnaire for Developing Countries, Lessons from 15 Years of the Living Standards Measurement Study,* Vol. I, The World Bank, Washington, D. C.

Grossman, M. and L. Benham, (1974), 'Health, Hours and Wages', in Perlman, M. (eds.), *The Economics of Health and Medical Care,* Macmillan and Co., London.

Gulati A., M. Svendson and N.R. Choudhury (1994), 'Major and Medium Irrigation Schemes-Towards Better Financial Management', *Economic and Political Weekly,* Vol. 29, No.26, pp.A72–A79.

UNDP (1999), *Human Development Report,* Oxford University Press, New York

Hobsbawm, Eric (1995), *The Age of Extremes: The Short Twentieth Century 1914–1991,* Abacus, London.

ICAR (1988), *Report of the ICAR Review Committee*, Indian Council of Agricultural Research, New Delhi.

ICAR (1995), *Report of the Committee on Partnership, Resource Generation, Training Consultancy, Contract Research/Contract Service, and Incentives and Reward System*, Indian Council of Agricultural Research, New Delhi.

Joshi, V. and I.M.D. Little (1994), *India: Macroeconomics and Political Economy*, The World Bank, Washington D.C.

Joshi, V. and I.M.D. Little (1996), *India's Economic Reforms 1991–2001*, Claredon Press, Oxford.

Krueger, A.O. (ed.) (1998), *The WTO As An International Organization*, Oxford University Press, New Delhi.

Kumar, P. and M.W. Rosegrant (1994), 'Productivity and Sources of Growth for Rice in India', *Economic and Political Weekly*, Vol. 29, No. 53, pp.A183–A188.

Lall, S. (2002), 'Transnational Corporations and Technology Flows', D. Nayyar (ed.), *Governing Globalization: Issues and Institutions*, Oxford University Press, New Delhi.

Leibenstein, Harvey (1957), *Economic Backwardness and Economic Growth: Studies in Theory and Economic Development*, John Wily Sons, New York.

Luft, H. S. (1975), "The Impact of Poor Health on Earnings", *The Review of Economics and Statistics*, Vol. 57, No.1, pp.43–57.

Meier, G.M. and J.E. Rauch (2000): *Leading Issues in Economic Development*, Seventh Edition, Oxford University Press, New York.

Misra, R., R. Chatterjee, and S. Rao (2003), *India Health Report*, Oxford University Press, New Delhi.

Mittar, V., Sukhwinder Singh, and J.S. Brar (2002), *Changing Structure of Education in Punjab: Some Issues and Policy Recommendations*, Publication Bureau, Punjabi University, Patiala.

Mushkin, S.J. (1962), 'Health as Investment', *Journal of Political Economy*, Vol. 70, No. 5, pp.129–157.

Nayyar, D. (1995), 'Globalization: The Past in Our Present', *Indian Economic Journal*, Vol. 43, No. 3, pp.1–18.

Nayyar, D. (1995), *Economic Liberalization in India: Analytics, Experience and Lessons*, Orient Longman, Calcutta.

Nayyar, D. and A. Sen (1994), 'International Trade and Agricultural Sector in India', in G.S. Bhalla (ed.), *Economic Liberalization and Indian Agriculture*, ISID-FAO, New Delhi.

Noss, A. (1991), 'Education and Adjustment: A Review of Literature', *Working Paper Series-701*, The World Bank, Washington, D.C.

Nurkse, R. (1953), *Capital Formation in Underdeveloped Countries*, Oxford University Press, New York.

Pal, S. and Alka Singh (1997), 'Agricultural Research and Extension in India: Institutional Structure and Investment', *Policy Paper-7*, National Centre for Agricultural Economics and Policy Research, (NCAEPR), New Delhi.

Pal, S. and R. Saxena (2003), 'Agricultural R & D Reforms in India: Policy and Institutional Imperatives', in S. Pal, Mruthyunjaya, P. K. Joshi and R. Saxena (eds.), *Institutional Change in Agriculture*, National Centre for Agricultural Economics and Policy, New Delhi, pp.181–204.

Prakash, G. and D. Raj (1972), 'Centre-State Relationship in the Field of Health and Family Welfare', in S. N. Jain, S. C. Kashyap, N. Srinivasan, and M. C. Shah (eds.), *The Union and States*, National Publishing House, Delhi.

Patnaik, P. and V. Rawal, (2005), 'Level of Activity in an Economy with Free Capital Mobility', *Economic and Political Weekly*, Vol. XL, No. 14, pp.1449–1457.

Paul, S., S. Balakrishan, K. Gopakumar, S. Sekhar, and M. Vivekananda (2004), 'State of India's Public Services: Benchmarks for the States', *Economic and Political Weekly*, Vol. 39, No. 9, pp.920–933.

Planning Commission (1999), *Ninth Five Year Plan 1997–2002*, Vol. II, Government of India, New Delhi.

Planning Commission (2002), *Tenth Five Year Plan 2002–2007*, Vol. II, Government of India, New Delhi.

Planning Commission (2003), *Punjab Development Report*, (prepared by CRRID, Chandigarh), Government of India, New Delhi.

Qadeer, I. (2000), 'Health Care Systems in Transition III, India, Part I—The Indian Experience', *Journal of Public Health Medicine*, Vol. 22, No. 1.

Rosenstein-Rodan, and N. Paul (1943), 'Problems of Industrialization of Eastern and South Eastern Europe', *Economic Journal*, Vol. 53, No. 210/211, pp.202–11.

Singh, Sukhwinder (1991), *Development and Use of Healthcare Services in Rural Areas: A Case Study of Punjab*, Unpublished Ph. D. Thesis, Department of Economics, Punjabi University, Patiala.

Singh, Sukhwinder (2005), 'Rural Health Infrastructure in Indian Punjab: Some Issues, Challenges and Policy Prescriptions', in Gopal Singh and R.K. Chauhan (eds.), *South Asia Today*, Anamika Publishers & Distributors (P) Ltd, New Delhi, pp.380–403.

Sodersten, B. (1970), *International Economics*, Macmillan, London.

Srinivasan, T.N. (2002), *Eight Lectures on India's Economic Reforms*, Oxford University Press, New Delhi.

Stiglitz, J. (2002), *Globalization and Its Discontents*, W.W. Norton and Company, New York.

Stiglitz, J. (2003), *Roaring Nineties: Seeds of Destruction*, Penguin Books, London.

Strauss, J. and T. Duncan (1995), 'Human Resources: Empirical Modeling of Household and Family Decisions', in J. Behrman and T.N. Srinavasan, (eds.), *Handbook of Development Economics*, North-Holland, Amsterdam.

Sulaiman, R. and G. Holt (2004), 'Extension, Poverty and Vulnerability in India', in Ian Christoplos and John Farsington (eds.), *Poverty, Vulnerability and Agricultural Extension: Policy Reforms in a Globalizing World*, Oxford University Press, New Delhi.

Tilak, J.B.G. (1996), 'How free is Free Education in India?' *Economic and Political Weekly*, Vol. 31, No.5 & 6, pp.275–282.

Tilak, J.B.G. (2004), 'Public Subsidies in Education in India', *Economic and Political Weekly*, Vol. 39, No. 4, pp.343–359.

Todaro, M.P. (1985): *Economic Development in the Third World*, Orient Longman, New Delhi.

Upendranadh C. (1993), 'Structural Adjustment and Education: Issues Related to Equity', *Economic and Political Weekly*, Vol. 28, No. 44, pp.2415–2419.

Vashishtha, P. S. (2005), 'Input Subsidies in Punjab Agriculture', Paper Presented, National Seminar on *Rationalizing Investment and Subsidies in Indian Agriculture*, Organized by CRRID, Chandigarh, 09–10 April.

Vernon, R. (1971), *Sovereignty at Bay*, Penguin Books, London.

Walle, D. and K. Nead (1995), *Public Spending and the Poor: Theory and Evidence*, The Johns Hopkins University Press, Baltimore, Maryland.

WHO (1996), *Equity in Health and Health Care-A WHO/SIDA Initiative*, World Health Organisation, Geneva.

World Bank (1993), *World Development Report: Investing in Health*, Oxford University Press, New York.

World Bank (1997), *Primary Education in India*, IBRD, Washington D.C.

World Bank (2004), *Punjab Development Report*, Poverty Reduction and Economic Management Sector Unit, South Asia Region, 26 June, IBRD, Washington D.C.

Wulf, L. D. (1975), 'Fiscal Incidence Studies in Developing Countries, Survey and Critique', *IMF Staff Papers*, Vol. 22, No.1, pp.61–131.

You, Joung-I L. (2002), 'The Bretton Woods Institutions: Evolution, Reform and Change', in Deepak Nayyar (ed.), *Governing Globalization-Issues and Institutions*, Oxford University Press, New Delhi, pp.209–237.